WHICH DECORATED STONEWARE JAR WILL BE THE FIRST TO SELL FOR $100,000.00?

SPECIAL THANKS

The authors want to extend special thanks to the following people for their assistance and cooperation.

Wayne Arthur Auctioneers, Hughesville, Pa.	Mason County Museum, Maysville, Ky.
Gordon Baker, Rockville, Md.	Maysville Kentucky Library, Maysville, Ky.
Bud Behm Auctioneers, Waynesburg, Pa.	Helen Mlinarcik, Masontown, Pa
D. Gregory Bott, Winchester, Va.	JoAnn Nicholson, Morgantown, W.Va.
B. Boggs, Maysville, Ky.	Palko Antiques, McClellandtown, Pa.
George Christy, Loretto, Pa.	Michael Pell, Uniontown, Pa.
Clara Bell Antiques, Zanesville, Oh.	David Powers, Cheshire, Oh.
D.H. Cochran, Waynesburg, Pa.	Joe Pyle Auctioneers, Mt. Morris, Pa.
Cookie Coombs, Morgantown, W.Va	Lantz and Marie Reppert, Yorktown, Pa.
Elvin Culp, Zanesville, Oh.	Richland Antiques, Gibsonia, Pa.
Michael Culp, Zanesville, Oh.	Wylie Rittenhouse, Auctioneer, Uniontown, Pa.
Alan H. Darby, Washington, D.C.	Riverbend Auction Co., Organ Cave, W.Va.
Merle Darrock, Bealsville, Pa.	Jerry and Jeanne Shobe, Winchester, Va.
Thomas C. Davidson, Pittsburgh, Pa.	Winchester Antiques, Winchester, Va.
Chris Dugan, McClellandtown, Pa.	Frank Swala, Jefferson, Pa.
John Eastwood, Danville, Va.	Thomas Pottery Company, Fredericktown, Pa.
Fox's Antiques, Butler, Pa.	T. Tyler Thompson Jr., Lexington, Ky.
Faye Free, Greensburg, Pa.	Beth and Earl Trimble, Leesburg, Pa.
Gene Green, Confluence, Pa.	Gary Trott, Fallston, Md.
German-Masontown Public Library, Masontown, Pa.	Varga's Antiques, Dave and Bonnie Wargo, Brier Hill, Pa.
Roger Jackson Auctions, Batavia, N.Y.	Vickie and Bruce Waasdorp, Clarence, N.Y.
Fred and Althea Kowalo, McDonald, Pa.	J.S. Williams, Dayton, Oh.
Loren Lambert, Parsons, W.Va.	George Wood House Antiques, Maysville, Ky.

America's Cobalt Decorated Stoneware

• SPECIAL EDITION •

BY DR. CARMEN A. GUAPPONE & MARIE A. GUAPPONE

Unusual 20 Gallon, Very Rare
$100,000.00

BOOK III: A PICTORIAL REFERENCE PRICE GUIDE

America's Cobalt Decorated Stoneware
• SPECIAL EDITION •

BY DR. CARMEN A. GUAPPONE & MARIE A. GUAPPONE

BOOK III
A Pictorial Reference Price Guide

■

Published and Distributed by:
Guappone Publishers
RD #1 Box 10
McClellandtown, PA 15458
(412) 737-5172

■

Owners:
Dr. Carmen A. Guappone
Marie A. Guappone
Susan C. Guappone
Anne C. Guappone

■

Additional copies may be ordered from:
Guappone Publishers
RD #1 Box 10
McClellandtown, PA 15458

■

Photographs by:
Marie A. Guappone
and others

■

Design, Typography & Production by:
Ron Guappone
10079-2 Windstream Drive
Columbia, MD 21044-2546
(410) 992-6743

■

Editors:
Susan C. Guappone
Anne C. Guappone

■

Special Aide:
Karl Guappone

■

© Copyright 1992
ISBN 0-9615230-3-4

12 Gallon Boughner
Greensboro, PA
$15,000

TABLE OF CONTENTS

Preface	7
Development of Decorated Stoneware	9
Stoneware and Tanware	10
Southwestern, Pa.	11
Shenandoah Valley Pottery	43
Stoneware Glazes	53
Maysville Pottery	54
Jane Lew Pottery	58
Northeastern United States	61
West Virginia	77
Jugs	79
Miscellaneous Potters	91
Conserving Your Pottery	94
Original Stoneware Price List	96
Future Prices of Crocks	97

Dedication

Dedicated to the
553 M.P.E.G.
1st Army
European Theater of War
World War II

In memory of those who have made the supreme sacrifice.

The 553 M.P.E.G. has met each year since 1946 on Labor Day.
The age of most members of this group was eighteen upon entrance into the service.
They served with pride and devotion for the United States of America.

1991 Reunion – New Oxford, Pennsylvania

PREFACE

Since I published my last book four years ago, the number of stoneware collectors has greatly increased. I attended many auctions and met collectors whom I have spoken to on the phone, which certainly is a pleasant experience. It is nice to answer their questions and talk about what types of jars we like to collect. One problem that exists for collectors, new and old, is the fact there is not much written material to help collectors learn about stoneware. Almost everyday, I learn of new stoneware-producing kilns. I am also surprised at the rate of increase in the value of stoneware. It is becoming more valuable everyday.

One reason the price of decorated stoneware has increased in value is that now more women are becoming serious collectors. They decorate their homes or offices in an early American decor. There is nothing more attractive than a beautiful jar in any room of your home. It definitely adds to the attractiveness of the room, especially 12, 16, or 20 gallon jars.

Most early collectors were men who enjoyed buying cobalt decorated jars and jugs. Their wives began to use them as containers for odds and ends, not really noticing their beauty, but later beginning to admire them. So now we have husband and wife collectors.

This created a much larger buying population. There are many different ways to collect decorated stoneware. Some people like to collect any piece of stoneware that is decorated with cobalt, either freehand or stenciled. Many collectors only collect advertising jars. Others collect jars from different potteries or potters. Some collect large jars, others only small jars.

able as a collector. You will be more selective and therefore will purchase more beautiful and expensive pottery.

There are a number of people who like to collect stoneware from local kilns. At one auction I attended, a common jar was being sold and most collectors thought it would sell for about $200.00. When the hammer fell, it sold for $900.00 and of course most people were surprised. When I asked the buyer why she paid such a high price, she stated that the jar was from her hometown and she was aware of only twelve in existence.

One observation I want to point out is that most collectors like to collect brushed free-hand deco-

Edmands & Co.
2 Gallon Crock
Stylized Bird in Foilage
$2500.00

rated stoneware. We should begin to acknowledge the fact that stencil decorated stoneware is also very creative and beautiful.

I want to also bring to your attention the practice of deciding who decorated the jar. Was it a woman or a man? A hunter, a fisherman, or a farmer? Were they left or right handed? An apprentice or an expert? To whom did the decorator try to appeal?-the male, female, or advertiser?

There are many things to learn when looking at the decorator's design and ability to decorate. Take notice of the cobalt. It seems some potters had excellent mixtures of cobalt and when fired they were very attractive. Some potters were skimpy and sloppy with their decorating and used very little cobalt. You wonder why a decorator or producer would do such a sloppy job when they were decorating to attract a buyer. In collecting you become aware of stencil and free-hand designs and their affect on the value of stoneware.

It is well known that any jar with scenes of birds, animals, fish, or just curved lines increased the value of any decorated jar. Collectors also place a great value on scratched decorations on stoneware jars.

Stoneware jars decorated only with stripes are beginning to increase in price. A few years ago, you could buy one for about $15.00. For some reason they began to escalate in price. Now the price range is from $30.00 to $200.00. It may be because they were inexpensive at first. Now all collectors are finding them attractive. Many of the small canning jars were decorated with stripes and women began decorating their kitchens with these small jars. Small jars set in some nook or cranny are attractive and adds to the decor of the home. Women began buying them and the demand increased and the value soared.

I must also comment on the increased value of the undecorated stoneware jars. They are increasing in value very fast. So you may want to consider putting a few away as an investment. Most of you remember when the plain or undecorated small jars sold for $5.00 or $7.00 and now they are selling for $25.00 and $35.00 a jar. I am quoting Southwestern Pennsylvania prices. Usually our prices reflect the same as in other areas.

I live about eight miles from New Geneva and Greensboro. These two towns manufactured thousands and thousands of stoneware pieces. New Geneva and Greensboro are both located on the Monongahela River in Southwestern Pennslyvania and manufactured the best blue stoneware in the United States. It was either brushed free-hand or decorated by stencil or a combination of both. The brushed free-hand decorated stoneware was exceptional. It is equal or better than any brushed decorated stoneware in the United States. I also believe that the slip cup quill decorated stoneware from Northeastern United States is of great beauty also.

The more you become interested in collecting stoneware, the more you appreciate its beauty. As you collect, take notice of the design and artistic quality.

In some books I autograph, I write "Buy Mint." Perhaps I should rewrite that statement concerning cracked and chipped jars. This statement applies to jars that are of common character and can generally be found at auctions. To give you an example, I recently purchased a cracked jar. It was very attractive and desirable wax sealer that measured about six inches tall and four inches wide at the base. Near the top it had two straight lines and then two

3 Gallon Crock
Starburst
T. Harrington
Lyons
$2700.00

bunches of cherries each containing three cherries and two leaves, all in beautiful cobalt. However, it had a hairline crack toward the back. I intended to buy it whatever the price. It was rare and unusual jar and one I would be proud to display in my home. Any collector would want to own this jar. You will see it pictured in this book.

For many years I have advocated that collectors not purchase cracked jars. Perhaps this thought must be revised. Most old cracked jars I have seen were not exceptional therefore no desire to own them was created. Now that I have seen one, my thinking has changed. I now believe that if the brushed or stenciled jar is very desirable, buy it if you like the design. In after thought, I have not seen a cracked crock that didn't sell. So it must depend on the price. At sales many auctioneers will say, "turn the cracked side to the wall and no one will know."

I have often told people, "If you like it, buy it!" In fact, I often autograph books with that bit of advice. I am a firm believer in buying what you like even if it means paying a higher price than what you may have intended. It is not good practice to go to a sale with a firm decision to pay only a certain price for a decorated stoneware jar, then when the auctioneer reaches that price, you stop bidding. I recommend that if you like it buy it. After all, we collect stoneware because we like it. If it is the type of crock that makes you want to take it home, buy it. You will never regret it, and you will be pleased forever.

— Dr. Carmen A. Guappone

Development Of Decorated Stoneware

Pottery was first made of red clay, and fired at a low temperature. It was porous and easily broken. Because of this it needed to be glazed. The glaze was made from clay and a mixture of lead. Pots were dipped in the glaze mixture before they were fired. However, this type of glaze caused lead poisoning. Many users of pottery became ill or even died as a result of eating food stored in lead-glazed stoneware.

The good stoneware clay came from Southwestern Pennsylvania and New Jersey. This produced a beautiful grey clay that could be fired at high temperatures. Since this grey clay did not require the lead-type glaze, food could be safely stored in these jars for long periods of time.

At first, stoneware was not decorated. Potters began decorating stoneware to make them more attractive to the buyer. They catered to both male and female buyers with the incised and brushed decorations. The artist's background and environment influenced his designs and decorations on various pieces of stoneware. These designs have caused the values of pottery to escalate thousands of dollars.

Early potters used a sharp stick or anything pointed to scratch a design on the surface of stoneware jars. Later, potters used cobalt to brush either straight or curved lines to obtain beautiful designs.

Most pottery at that time cost about ten cents a gallon, but eventually pottery became valuable because of its design. When pottery became more desirable because of its decoration, the demand increased. This caused more elaborate designs to be created on stoneware jars. Today these outstanding designs are prized by collectors and valued in the thousands of dollars.

One of the developments that I have not discussed is the use of one or more stencils in decorating stoneware. I suggest you look at your prized collection and decide how many stencils were used to design your stoneware jars. You should also become aware that designing a stencil is also creative. Many stencils are exceptional in their design. I consider the stenciled design on stoneware jars as part of the attraction, because it gives the collector more opportunities to collect unusual designs of stoneware. It also adds another dimension to collecting. Stencils are designs created in the artist's mind.

I would suggest that you do not limit yourself to collecting only brushed or stenciled designs, or only specific sizes and shapes of jars. This will certainly contain your collection. If you see a stoneware jar that creates a strong desire for you to own it, then buy it, even if the price is more than you want to pay. It will take only a few months until the value surpasses what you paid for it. Remember, there are nicer things to have than money.

Wax Sealer
Freehand & Stencil
One Gallon
$750.00

"If you like it, buy it!" This is a belief that I have and I follow It. If the crock makes you want to own it, then it has the same affect on other collectors, therefore it has a greater value. It is easier to acquire money than a beautiful designed cobalt stoneware jar.

Stoneware And Tanware

Freehand
1866
$4000.00

N. Clark Lyons
2 Gallon Cream Pot
Starburst Design
$6000.00

Stoneware and tanware was manufactured in New Geneva and Greensboro, Pennsylvania. These towns are located on the Monongahela River which flows between both villages. New Geneva is in Fayette County and Greensboro is in Greene County both in Southwestern Pennsylvania.

New Geneva was founded by Albert Gallatin, the second treasurer of the United States. He was from Geneva, Switzerland. New Geneva manufactured tanware, stoneware, wagons, guns (rifles), glassware, and farm implements. A packet sidewheeler from Pittsburgh, Pa. regularly stopped at New Geneva to drop off needed iron, steel, gunpowder, and other farm and household items.

On the return trip to Pittsburgh, the packet sidewheeler was loaded with guns, glassware, farm implements, and produce. But, most importantly, hundreds of gallons of stoneware pottery. Stoneware was a major product and this utilitarian folk pottery was transported to towns all along the Monongahela, Ohio, and Mississippi Rivers, and on to its final stop, New Orleans.

Greensboro, just across the river from New Geneva, also produced stoneware. Both villages produced stoneware, including wax sealers, canning jars, butter churns, butter bowls, and all sorts of pottery, from whiskey and molasses jugs to large stoneware containers. This would amount to several hundred thousand gallons of stoneware each year.

Debolt began producing stoneware in New Geneva in 1849, and production continued until 1916. Greensboro began producing in about 1810, but because of a fire, stopped around the turn of the century, 1896.

SOUTHWESTERN PA.

Freehand Brushed Jar
2 Gallon
$295.00

15 Gallon Crock
Star Pottery
Hamilton & Jones
Greensboro, Pa.
$20,000.00

Advertising Storage Crock
Moser Bros., McLellandtown (misspelled), Pa.
Eagle Design, 6 Gallon
Eagle Pottery
Rare, $7000.00

Brandy Keg
Pig Shaped, Very Rare
$12,000.00

Isaac Hewitt, Jr.
Rices Landing, Pa.
Excelsior Works
$2500.00

James Hamilton & Co.
Greensboro, Pa.
1 Gallon, 10" Height
$295.00

E.S. & B.
New Brighton, Pa.
2 Gallon, 11" Height
$200.00

Hamilton & Jones
Greensboro, Pa.
3 Gallon
$1100.00

Samuel Cooper
Pittsburgh, Pa.
$295.00

James Hamilton & Co.
Greensboro, Pa.
$895.00

Freehand Jar
Floral Decor
$500.00

Hamilton & Jones
Greensboro, Pa.
$750.00

James Hamilton & Co.
Greensboro, Pa.
Stencilled Shield
$900.00

James Hamilton & Co.
Greensboro, Pa.
$695.00

Shield
$650.00

A. Conrad
New Geneva, Pa.
$450.00

James Hamilton & Co.
Greensboro, Pa.
$395.00

Freehand Brushed Jar
$450.00

Freehand Brushed Jar
$295.00

C.L. Williams
New Geneva, Pa.
2 Gallon
$700.00

4 Gallon Jar (14½")
Hamilton & Co.
Greensboro, Pa.
$4000.00

Stenciled Jar
5 Gallon, 15" Height
$800.00

16

Storage Jar
2 Gallon
$200.00

1839 Jar
$690.00

A.P. Donaghho
Parkersburg, W.Va.
4 Gallon
$225.00

12 Gallon Crock
Boughner
$15,000.00

Demuth's Snuff
Lancaster, Pa.
$195.00

Hamilton & Jones
Star Pottery
Greensboro, Pa.
Stencilled
$895.00

Crock (15")
James Hamilton & Co.
Greensboro, Pa.
$20,000.00

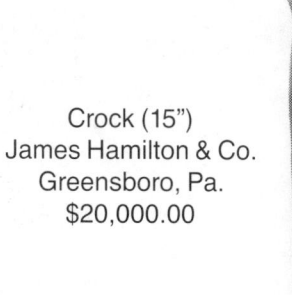

4 Gallon Crock
Eagle Pottery
T.F. Reppert
Greensboro, Pa.
$4000.00

Batter Jug
4 Gallon
$600.00

A.P. Donaghho
Parkersburg, W.Va.
1/2 Quart, 6" Height
$595.00

Freehand
6 Gallon
$1500.00

Freehand
3 Gallon
$850.00

Hamilton & Jones
Greensboro, Pa.
Storage Jar
3 Gallon
$895.00

John Weaver
$625.00

E. Fowler
Beaver, Pa.
5 Gallon
$350.00

L.B. Dilliner
New Geneva, Pa.
Eagle - Rare
Freehand and Stencil
$2000.00

Cobalt Jar
2 Gallon, 9" Height
$800.00

19

Freehand, Cobalt
Dated 1840
$895.00

Crock
9" Height
$900.00

4 Gallon Crock
Dog Design
$50,000.00

R.T. Williams
New Geneva, Pa.
4 Gallon
$600.00

James Hamilton & Co.
Greensboro, Pa.
$800.00

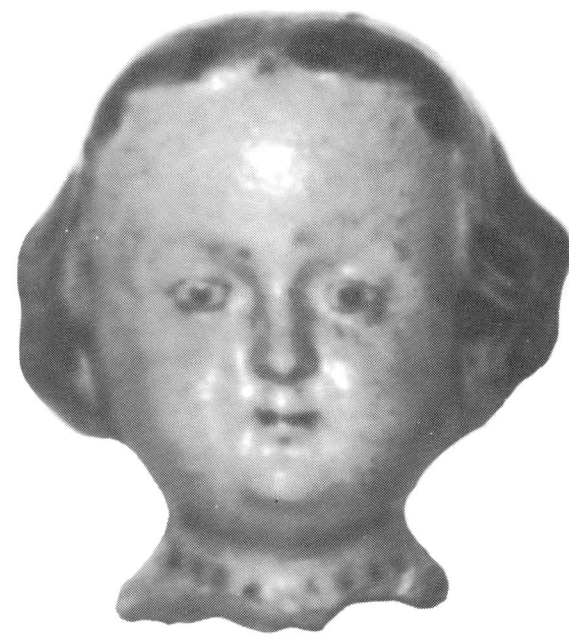

Stoneware Doll Head
New Geneva, Pa.
Rare: $8,000.00

James Hamilton & Co.
Greensboro, Pa.
3 Gallon
$800.00

16 Gallon
Water Cooler
$2200.00

Flower Pot (8")
Cobalt Flowers
Applied Buttons Around
Openwork Crown
$10,000.00

21

Stoneware Doll Head
New Geneva, Pa.
Rare: $8,000.00

James Hamilton & Co.
Greensboro, Pa.
Freehand, 3 Gallon
$325.00

Advertising Crock
Samuel Cooper
Pittsburgh, Pa.
Freehand & Stencil
Mint, $550.00

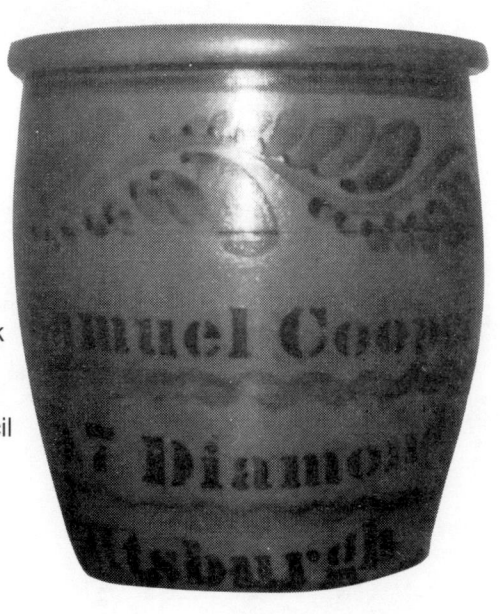

2 Gallon Jar (12")
James Hamilton
Eagle Pottery
Greensboro, Pa.
$3000.00

Dragonfly
$495.00

Hamilton & Jones
Greensboro, Pa.
$900.00

Freehand Decor
5 Gallon
$900.00

James Hamilton & Co.
Greensboro, Pa.
Shield
2 Gallon
$1500.00

Freehand Decor
4 Gallon
$950.00

New Geneva Pottery
Freehand & Stencil
1 1/2 Gallon
$900.00

Williams & Reppert
Greensboro, Pa.
Stoneware Pitcher
$2200.00

James Hamilton & Co.
Greensboro, Pa.
Water or Milk Pitcher
$2100.00

A.V. Boughner
Greensboro, Pa.
Pear Design
3 Gallon
$3000.00

A.V. Boughner
Greensboro, Pa.
Thistle Design
4 Gallon
$3000.00

W.B. Cooper & Bros.
10 Gallon
$1500.00

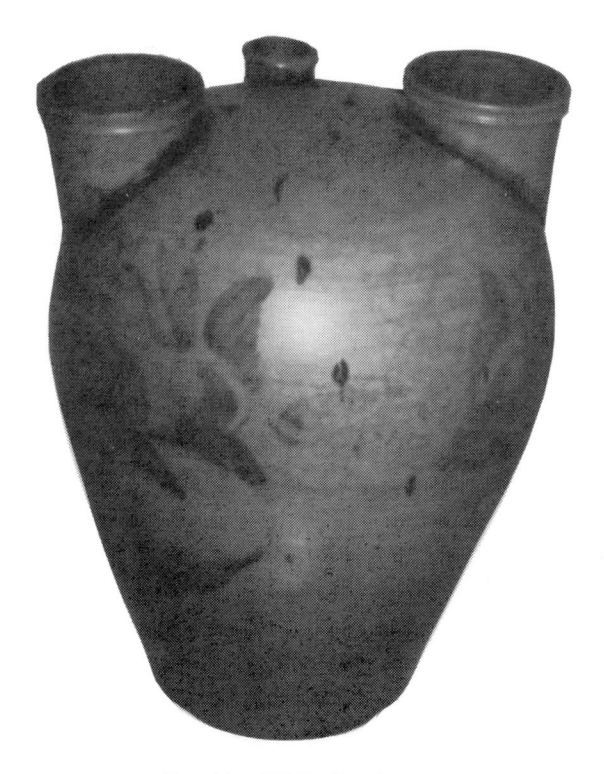

Freehand Tulip Design
$5000.00

Stoneware Pitcher
Freehand
$1800.00

Freehand & Stencil
2 Gallon
$900.00

J. Littel
Greensboro, Pa.
Very Rare
$2400.00

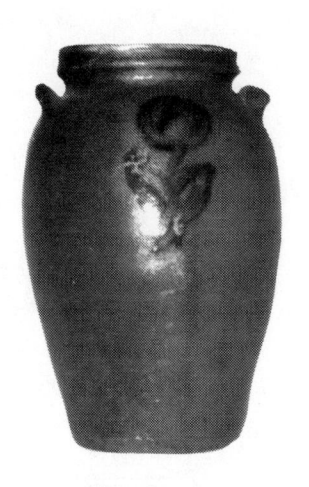

Freehand Flower Design
$900.00

Western Pa. Pitcher
2 Gallon, 13" Height
$1900.00

Pitcher
1 Gallon, 10" Height
$1200.00

Cobalt Flask
$900.00

James Hamilton & Co.
Greensboro, Pa.
Mint, 5 Gallon
$900.00

New Geneva Pottery
4 Gallon
$950.00

Freehand Decor
Western, Pa. Jar
4 Gallon
$700.00

Crock
13" Height
$200.00

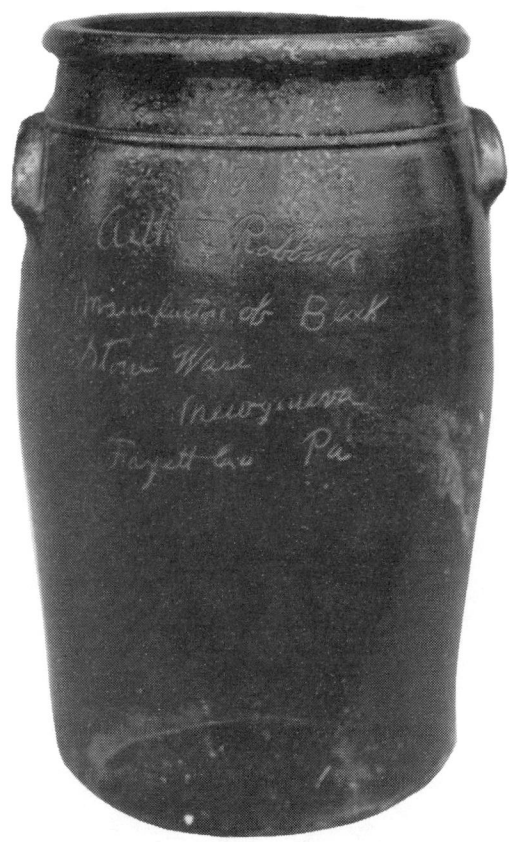

10 Gallon Jar (20 1/2")
Albany Slip Covered
Arthur Robbins
Manufacturer of "Black Stoneware"
Fayett (misspelled) Co., New Geneva, Pa.
$10,000.00

Freehand Decor
$850.00

James Hamilton & Co.
Greensboro, Pa.
$900.00

Small Jar
$895.00

Freehand Decor
$900.00

Hamilton & Jones
Greensboro, Pa.
Eagle, 20 Gallon
Mint, $8000.00

Storage Jar
Stephen H. Ward
West Brownsville, Pa.
Cobalt & Stencil
4 Gallon, $900.00

Freehand Decor
3 Gallon
$1200.00

Wax Sealer
Cobalt
Freehand & Stencil
$725.00

Hamilton & Jones
Star Pottery
Greensboro, Pa.
5 Gallon
$8000.00

Freehand Decor
4 Gallon
$800.00

James Hamilton & Co.
Greensboro, Pa.
Freehand - Cobalt
Dated 1852, 10 Gallon
$5000.00

Stripes & Two Horses
$875.00

2 Gallon Jar
$150.00

Hamilton & Jones
Star Pottery
Greensboro, Pa.
$800.00

Stripes & Cherries
$675.00

Wax Sealer
Cobalt
$695.00

Pig Bank
$4000.00

Hamilton & Jones
Cherries
$895.00

Cherries
Greensboro, Pa.
$895.00

Wax Sealer
1 Quart
$200.00

Isaac Hewitt, Jr.
Rices Landing, Pa.
$850.00

Jar with 5 Stripes
(6")
$595.00

Dog Doorstop (12")
Named "Charlie"
C.L. Williams
New Geneva, Pa.
$10,000.00

Harvest Jug (6")
$900.00

1 Quart Canner (6¼")
A. Conrad & Co.
$2500.00

1 Quart Canner (6¾")
Star Pottery
$2500.00

People Crock
6 Gallon
Rare/$30,000.00

Stripes
$695.00

Stripes
$595.00

Hamilton & Jones
Birds
Greensboro, Pa.
$295.00

People Crock
2 Quarts
Freehand Cobalt
$6000.00

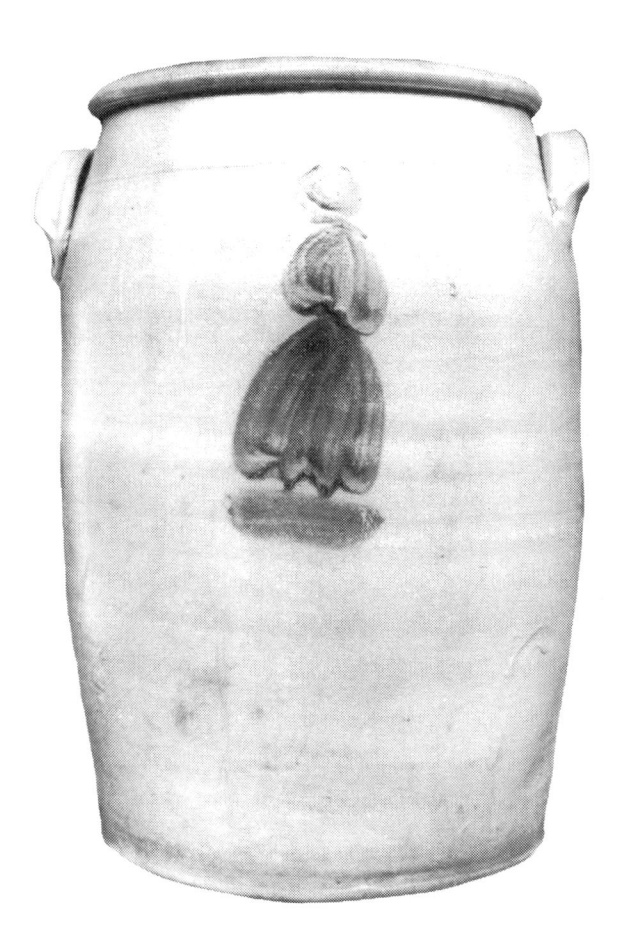

People Crock
$6000.00

Dog Door Stop
1892
$900.00

Pig Bank
$3000.00

People Crock
$7000.00

Greensboro, Pa.
Thistle
$1500.00

A. Conrad
Fayette Co.
New Geneva, Pa.
$295.00

Butter Crock (5")
$400.00

Crock
Bird Design
$1900.00

People Crock
$8000.00

Canning Jar (7")
Straight & Squiggle Lines
Double Cherries
$3000.00

Palatine Pottery Co.
Pear
Palatine W. Va.
$650.00

Conrad
New Geneva
$225.00

Palatine Pottery & Co.
Dog
Palatine, W. Va.
$795.00

Wax Sealer
Fayette Co., Pa.
$295.00

Pear
Palatine, W. Va.
$650.00

Mug with Dancing Lady
Robinson Clay Co.
Ohio
$150.00

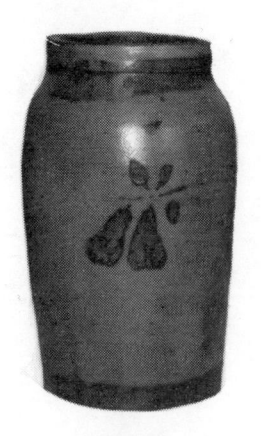

Pears
$750.00

Canning Jar (10")
Stripes
$200.00

Pears
Greensboro, Pa.
$795.00

Advertising Crock (8")
John A. Rathbone
Palestine, W. Va.
$400.00

Plums
$750.00

Wax Sealer
Samuel Cooper
Pittsburgh, Pa.
$900.00

Flask (6")
Cobalt Decoration
New Jersey
$1200.00

1 Quart Bottle
$150.00

Ink Well
$2000.00

Advertising Jar
1 Gallon
$350.00

Butter Crock (6")
1 Gallon
$300.00

Hamilton & Jones
Pears
Greensboro, Pa.
$825.00

Stoneware Jug
$300.00

1 Gallon Storage Jar
Cobalt Eagle Design
A.P. Donaghho
Fredericktown, Pa.
$1500.00

Advertising Jar, Two Eagles
W.F. Cooper & Bros., Pittsburgh, Pa.
Cobalt & Stencil
Eagle Pottery, Greensboro, Pa.
Rare, $20,000.00

Palatine Pottery
Pear
Palatine, W. Va.
$695.00

1 Quart jar
Stripes
$800.00

1 Quart Canner (6¼")
James Hamilton & Co.
$1000.00

Millers Potter
Racoon, W. Va.
$495.00

A.P. Donaghho
½ Gallon
Fredericktown, Pa.
Stenciled Cobalt
$800.00

Crock, 20 Gallon
Southern Ohio
$4000.00

R.C.R. 1860 (14")
Remney
Philadelphia
Freehand
$1400.00

Crock (19")
10 Gallon
James Hamilton & Co.
Greensboro, Pa.
$5000.00

Butter Churn
Drakes Reaction
Freehand Cobalt
$1500.00

Advertising Crock
20 Gallon
Rome, Indiana
$15000.00

Storage Jar
A.P. Donaghho
Federicktown, Pa.
$225.00

Canning Jar (10")
Stripes & Wavy Lines
$700.00

1 Quart Snuff Jar
$150.00

Crock (23")
16 Gallon
Freehand
$8000.00

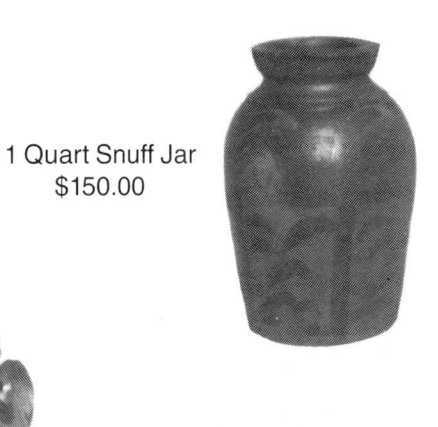

Crock (16")
Donaghho Co.
Parkersburg, W. Va.
$500.00

Flower Pot
$35.00

Crock (17")
12 Gallon
Union Stoneware Co.
Red Wing, Mn.
$250.00

Crock
Donaghho
10 Gallon
Parkersburg, W. Va.
$1500.00

Brandy Crock (16")
Freehand
$1200.00

Storage Jar
Freehand Cobalt
3 Gallon
$700.00

Lard Crock
Roses, 3 Gallon
$400.00

A.V. Boughner
Greensboro, Pa.
5 Gallon, 15 1/2" Height
$5000.00

Butter Jar
Freehand - Cobalt
Stars and Floral Design
3 Gallon
$800.00

Shenandoah Valley Pottery

by Marie A. Guappone

Peter Bell was the first important valley potter. He produced pottery in Hagerstown, Md. in 1805. He later moved to Winchester, Va. where he made mostly utilitarian earthware. Not many of his pieces were marked; but some were stamped "P. Bell." He died in Hagerstown in 1847 at age 72. Three of his sons became master potters. John, the oldest, was one the best potters of the valley. He worked in Waynesboro, Pa., Winchester, Va., and Chambersburg, Pa. He stamped his pottery with "J. Bell," later "John Bell," and still later "John Bell, Waynesboro."

Peter Bell's two other sons, Samuel Bell and Solomon Bell were both extraordinary potters. The Bell family made the greatest impact of all the potters in the Shenandoah Valley.

Anthony W. Baecher was one of the most masterful and skilled Shenandoah potters. He came to America in 1848. Baecher built a pottery in Winchester, Va. in 1868. Early pieces were stamped "Bacher," the Germanic spelling of his name. Later he used the stamp "Baecher, Winchester, Va," He was an extremely diversified potter. He used various appliques of birds, flowers, and leaves on his pottery. He was a master at pottery animals. As a creator of folk pottery sculpture, Baecher's contributions are indisputable.

Another important group of potters of the Shenandoah Valley was the Eberly Family. Jacob, who was not a potter, established a pottery in Strasburg in 1880. His son, Letcher, learned the craft and worked in the pottery. Eberly's chief employee was Theodore Fleet. The Eberly group consistently marked their objects. The first stamp used was "J. Eberly and Co., Strasburg, Va.," then "J. Eberly and Bro., Strasburg, Va.," then "From J. Eberly and Bro., Strasburg, Va.," the last "Eberly & Son, Strasburg, Va." The pottery ceased operations in 1906.

One of the lesser known potters of the lower Shenandoah Valley was John George Schweinfurt. In 1850 he established a pottery in New Market, Va., where he maninly produced earthenware, crocks, toys, pitchers, cups, banks, inkwells, and flower pots.

Pitcher and Bowl Set
with Rope Handles & Soap Dish
S. Bell & Son, c. 1870s
$7700.00

Other notable stoneware potters were Jeremiah Keister, Amos Keister, James M. Hickerson, Samuel H. Sonner, John H. Sonner, William H. Lehew, George W. Miller, W. H. Christman, and L. D. Funkhouser. All of these men worked various times between 1870 and 1906.

Stoneware

Most of the Shenandoah Valley folk pottery was earthenware. After refining the native clay, the potters began to make stoneware. Much of the stoneware had brushed decorations in cobalt blue and sometimes manganese brown. Their designs were tulips, other plant forms, or crude C-Scrolls. Many potters had favorite designs. Solomon Bell was fond of the lion motif. The Eberlys used a birdwing motif. Solomon and Samuel Bell also used the American eagle in their decorations. Another Bell characteristic is the hand - shaping of flower pots,

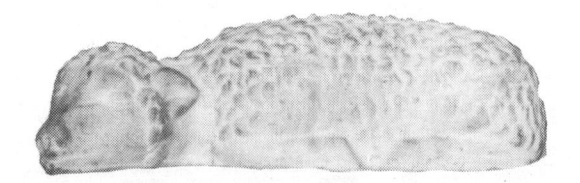

Lamb Doorstop
Bell (L: 11")
White Glaze
$5000.00

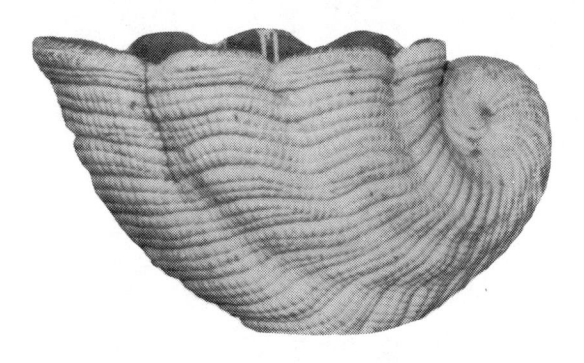

Sea Shell Planter
1880-1900 (11" x 20")
J. Eberly & Bro.
Pedestal Missing
White Slip $2600.00

small vases, and crocks in the form of a bell. Baecher applied leaves, flowers, and birds to his pottery pieces. Most of his flower pots have a double - scalloped and pinched rim. The Eberlys used more clay appliques than any of the other potters. They used motifs such as seashells, medallions, heads in relief; also molds of snakes, lizards, lions, lilies, roses, and daises. The Eberlys gave the valley some very outstanding pottery.

Glazes

One of the signature characteristics of Shenandoah Pottery is the multi-color glaze. This glaze was essentially a two-step process. Greenware earthenware objects, when in a biscuit (once-fired) state, were given an all-over coating of white slip, usually by dripping. The next step in the creation of the mottled glaze was the addition of various green (copper oxide) and/or various brown (manganese dioxide) glaze configurations that were created by brushing, sponging, spattering, dipping, dripping, or by holding the object in different positions to control the flow and path of the colored glaze. Sometimes, effects of the bleeding of the colored glaze into the white slip created many different colors. The next step was to use a lead overglaze to seal the object. It was said that after the Civil War, local boys would go out into the battlefields to collect lead bullets for sale to the potters for use in their glaze.

Salt glazing on cobalt decorated stoneware was the other type of glazing used in the Shenandoah Valley.

By 1908, all the potteries in the prolific Shenandoah Valley had closed.

■Taken in most part from:
Folk Pottery of the Shenandoah Valley, by William E. Wiltshire, III, Introduction by H.E. Comstock, Copyright 1975, E.P. Dutton & Co., Inc, New York, pp. 9-21

If you are interested in Shenandoah Pottery, stop at Winchester Antiques in Winchester, Va. They have Shenandoah Valley stoneware for your inspection and enjoyment.

Bell Shaped Flower Pot
(5") S. Bell & Son
$750.00

Small Flower Holder (3")
Multiglaze
$850.00

Bell Shaped
Flower Pot (5")
Bell, Multiglaze
$900.00

Pitcher (6")
Bell & Son
Strasburg, Va.
$2000.00

Pitcher (10")
Solomon Bell & Son
Strasburg, Va.
$2100.00

Baecher Flower Pot (7")
Winchester, Va.
Double Crimped
Mocha Chocolate Glaze
$890.00

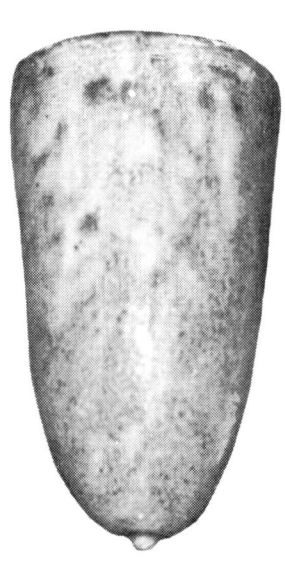

Wall Pocket (7")
Eberly
Strasburg, Va.
$300.00

Pitcher (10")
S. Bell & Son
Strasburg, Va.
Multiglaze, $1700.00

Hunt Scene Pitcher (8")
Solomon Bell
Multiglaze
$2300.00

Flower Pot (9")
S. Bell & Son
Multiglaze
$950.00

Basket (10")
E. Brown
North Carolina
$125.00

Milk Pitcher (5")
Illiterate Potter Signed
With House on Base
Covington, Va.
Blue Glaze, $200.00

Pitcher
Eberly
Strasburg
$1600.00

Mug (5")
S. Bell & Son
$975.00

Shenandoah Crock
(8") Damaged
$500.00

Baecher Pitcher (7")
Winchester, Va.
Brown Glaze
$1000.00

Bell Pitcher (6")
Multiglaze
$1350.00

Bell Pitcher (7")
Brown Glaze
$1300.00

Bell Pitcher (6")
Mocha Glaze
$1300.00

Pitcher (7")
S. Bell & Son
$2800.00

Egg Cup (4")
Strasburg, Va.
Multiglaze
$535.00

46

Spaniel (9")
Solomon Bell
$2100.00

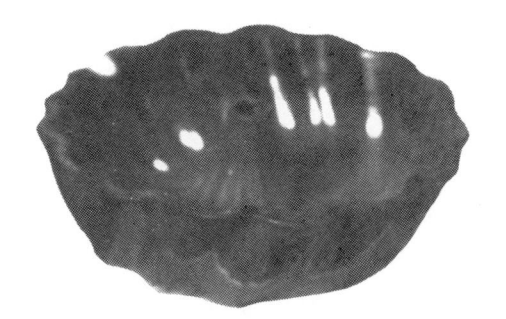

Cake Mold (9" Deep)
John Bell
Strasburg, Va.
$150.00

Dish (D-5")
Coffman
Brown Glaze
New Market, Va.
$65.00

S.H. Sonner (8")
$250.00

D.H. Hinkel (6")
"STONEY MAN"
Harrisonburg, Va.
and Luray, Va.
Signed Snuff Jar
Rare/$375.00

Pitcher (17")
Winchester Potters 1910
Brown Glaze
$1400.00

Flask
Height 5"
$900.00

L.D. Funkhouser (9")
Strasburg, Va. 1900
Advertisement on reverse
One of last known
potters in Strasburg
Rare/$500.00

Flower Pot (9")
Stoneware
Eberly & Bro.
Strasburg, Va.
$200.00

Bean Pot (9")
Eberly & Co.
Strasburg, Va.
$325.00

Smith (Width: 8")
Alexandria, Va.
Lincoln Drape Cobalt
$400.00

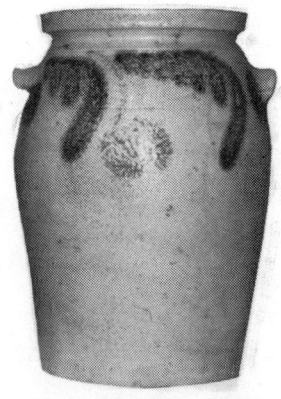

Early Solomon Bell
(10") Freehand Cobalt
$800.00

J.M. Hickerson (6")
Strasburg, Va.
Freehand Cobalt
$350.00

Shenandoah Valley (13")
Thistle Design
Cobalt Decoration
$2200.00

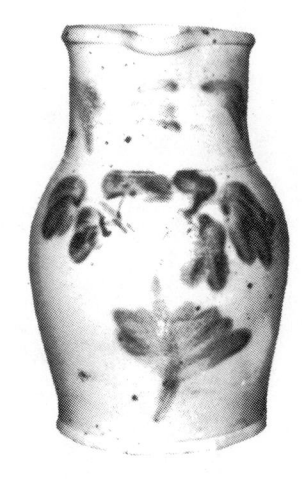

Pitcher (10")
3/4 Gallon, Pa.
Heavy Cobalt Decoration
$2000.00

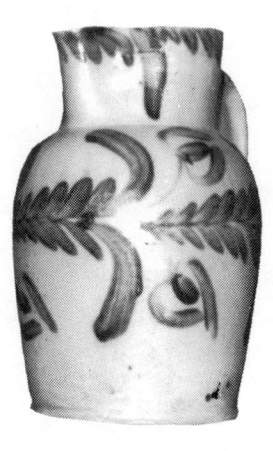

Pitcher (11")
$2800.00
Origin Unkown

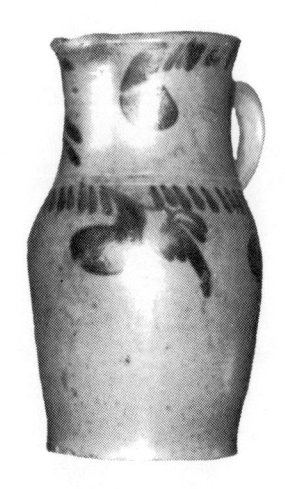

Pitcher (13")
Eberly
Freehand
Strasburg, Va.
$3000.00

Pitcher (11")
1 Gallon
$5500.00

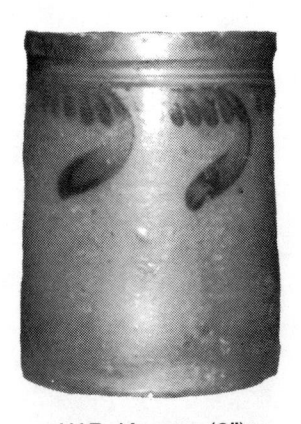

W.B. Kenner (9")
Signed
Strasburg, Va. 1880
One Gallon
$400.00

Pitcher (11")
Shenandoah Valley
Cobalt Decoration
$1400.00

48

Shenandoah Valley (9")
Freehand Tulips
Cobalt
$300.00

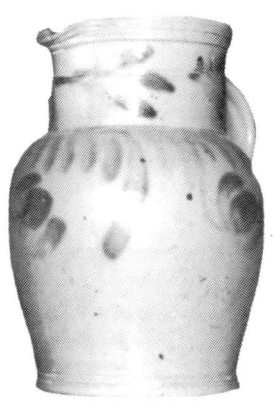

Pitcher (11")
S. Bell
$2100.00

Stoneware Pitcher (5")
Shenandoah Valley
$2600.00

Spitton
Bell
Strasburg, Va.
$395.00

Storage Jar (17")
Fowler, 5 Gallon
$795.00

Solomon Bell (14")
Strasburg, Va.
Freehand Tulip
$495.00

B.C. Millburn (11")
Alexander, Va.
Freehand Cobalt
$895.00

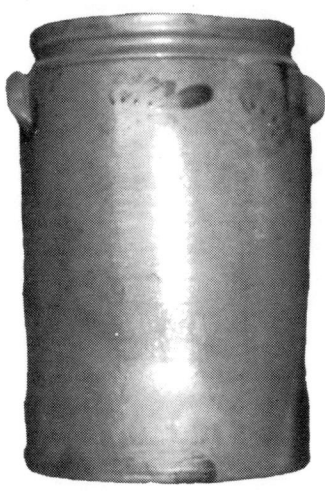

Theophilus Grim (15")
Shenandoah Valley
3 Gallon
Rare/$695.00

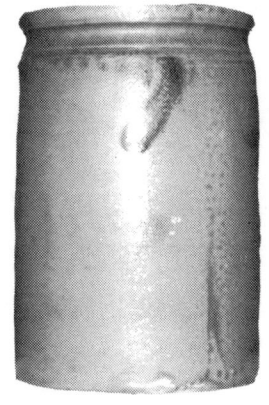

Miller & Woodware (10")
Signed
Strasburg, Va.
One Gallon
$350.00

Smith (15")
Washington, D.C.
Rope Handles
Freehand Cobalt
$2500.00

49

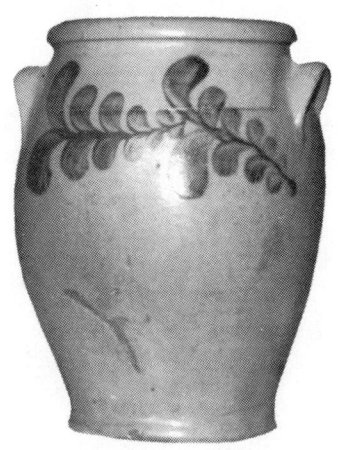

J. Miller (12")
1st Potter in
Strasburg, Va.
Freehand Cobalt
Rare/$2000.00

W.H. Lehew (11")
Strasburg, Va.
$2200.00

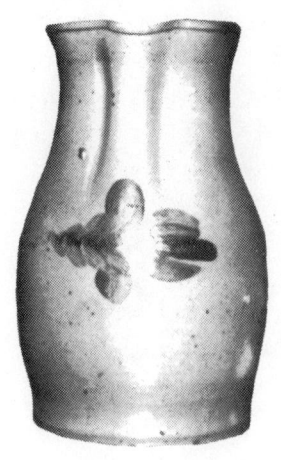

Pitcher (11")
Attributed to E. Sutter
One Gallon
$1500.00

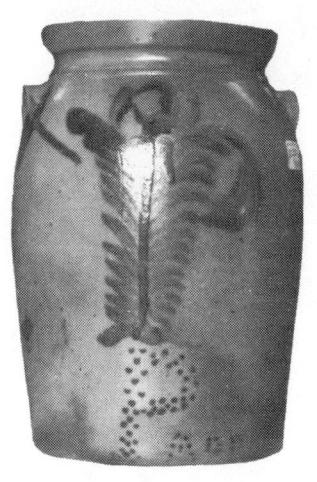

Crock
Signed Parr
Richmond, Va.
Cobalt Flower
$700.00

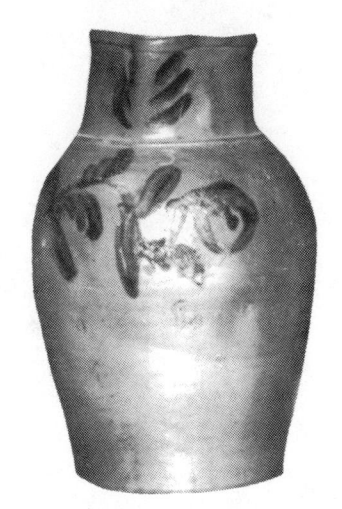

Pitcher (17")
3 Gallon
Strasburg, Va.
$900.00

Pitcher (11")
W.H. Lehew & Co
Strasburg, Va.
$1700.00

G.N Fulton (17")
2 Gallon (Damaged)
Cobalt Decorated
$295.00

Milk Bowl (7")
S. Bell
One Handle Only
Freehand Cobalt
$500.00

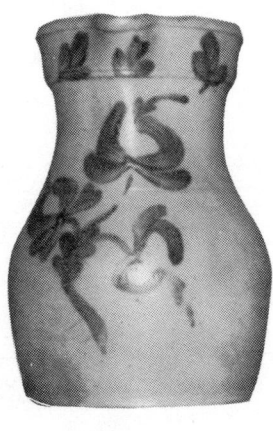

Pitcher (11")
Swank
Johnstown, Pa.
Freehand Decoration
$2100.00

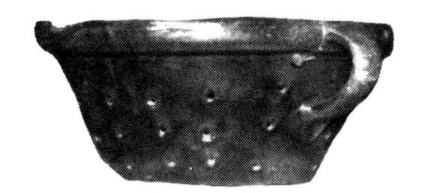

Colander (5")
Unknown
North Carolina
Rare/$1500.00

D.P. Haynes & Co. (12")
Crown Brand
Baltimore, Md.
2 Gallon, Stencil Design
$4000.00

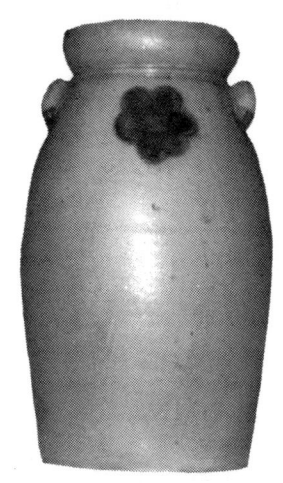

Butter Churn (15")
Early Shenandoah Valley
3 Gallon
Cobalt Daisy
$1600.00

Butter Churn (20")
Heatwole
Rockingham Co.
Harrison, Va.
$750.00

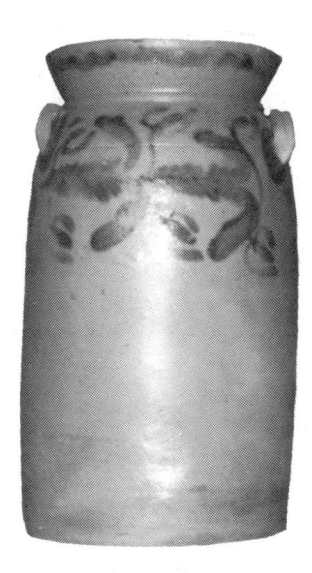

Butter Churn (17")
S. Bell
Shenandoah Valley
$2500.00

Jardiniere (12")
Freehand Tulip
Cobalt
$495.00

Pitcher
1½ Gallon
Richmond, Va.
$2100.00

Pie Saver (8")
Redware
Strasburg, Va.
$950.00

Bank (4")
Emmanuel Suter
Rockingham Co.
Harrisonburg, Va.
$495.00

Tree Stump Door Stop
Redware (8")
Strasburg, Va.
$165.00

Jug (10")
J. Keister & Co.
Strasburg, Va.
$325.00

Coffman (6")
New Market, Va.
Multiglaze
$185.00

Flue Pipe (10")
John Bell
$150.00

Sieve or Strainer
$2100.00

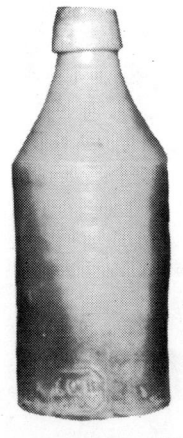

Remmey Soda (10")
Philadelpia, Pa.
R.C.R. Philadelpia, Pa.
$195.00

Flower Pot (6")
Redware
Double-crimped
$165.00

Pitcher (8")
Joliffe
Winchester, Va.
Dr. Green Glaze
Squiggle Incised Design
$800.00

Stoneware Glazes

Watercooler (14")
Solomon Bell
Freehand Tulips
$1200.00

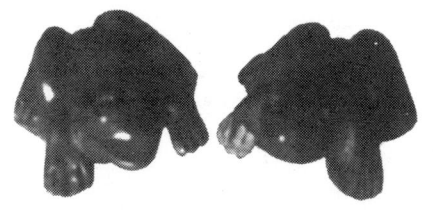

Whimsies (Male & Female Frog Set)
"Watt Cheer" 1890-1900
W.Va.-Ky. Line
$195.00 each

Cuspidor (6")
Bell
Multiglaze
$220.00

Umbrella Stand (20")
Eberly
Strasburg, Va.
$3000.00

The following formulas were taken from the book *The Shenandoah Pottery* by Rice and Stoudt. These formulas belonged to Lorenzo D. Fleet who learned throwing pottery and glazing in the Bell Brothers shops.

Permission was given by Theodore Fleet, son of Lorenzo D. Fleet, to A.H. Rice and John Baer Stoudt to publish these formulas in *The Shenandoah Pottery*.

Glazings by L.D. Fleet, Shenandoah Valley

Common Pot Glaze

6 measures of clay
9 measures of red led
1 pint of Pap

Green Glaze

10 measures red led
1 measure of copper skales
6 measures of white clay
1 pint of Pap

Brown Glaze

10 measures red led
1 measure of Magnees
6 measures of red clay
1 pint of Pap

Yellow Glaze

1 measures anvil dust
10 measure of red led
6 measures of white clay
1 pint of Pap

Maysville Pottery

Freehand & Stencil Pitcher
G.A. & J.E. McCarthey
Maysville, Ky.
$4000.00

Maysville, Ky., the county seat of Mason County, is situated on the south side of the Ohio River, on a high plateau at the mouth of the Limestone Creek.

One pottery is listed in the library records: Keith Bros. Limestone Pottery.

Isaac Thomas was listed as a potter residing in W. Maysville. This information was taken from the "Maysville City Directory and Business Mirror" for 1860-61.

Another Maysville potter was N. Copper, whose designs are similar to Southwestern Pennsylvania pottery. Some Collectors in Maysville, Ky. believe the stoneware was made and decorated in the New Geneva and Greensboro area and sent down by the packet boat to Kentucky. However, there is no evidence to substantiate this theory.

There are several Maysville, Ky. advertising jugs pictured in the book with the name M.C. Russell or M.C.R. on them. Another type of stoneware had the name C.W. Rodgers. It is not known whether these stoneware jugs were manufactured in Maysville.

G.A. & J.E. McCarthey are also significant names on Maysville pottery.

Highly decorated Maysville stoneware is beautiful, rare, expensive, and collectible.

Bierbower Stoves
Advertising Jar
Maysville, Ky. (8")
$800.00

M.C. Russell & Son
Advertising Jug (6")
Maysville, Ky.
$195.00

3 Gallon
G.A. & J.E. McCarthey
Maysville, Ky.
$15,000.00

Stoneware Bottle
M.C. Russell
Maysville, Ky.
$250.00

M.C.R. Advertising Jug
Maysville, Ky. (7")
$600.00

6 Gallon Butter Churn
Freehand
Maysville, Ky.
$7000.00

Butter Crock
Maysville (Ht: 5")
$2100.00

Freehand Decorated
Ht: 15"
$800.00

Quart Canning Jar
McCarthy (8")
Maysville, Ky.
$250.00

Jug (18")
Maysville
$250.00

Crock (Ht: 10")
McCarthey
Maysville, Ky.
$1500.00

G.A. & J.E. McCarthey
Maysville, Ky.
$3000.00

Rodgers Old Stock
Whiskey Jug (10")
Maysville, Ky.
$275.00

Omar Dodson
Lady's Whiskey Jug
Maysville, Ky. (8")
$275.00

M.C.R. Jug
Maysville (7")
$300.00

M.C. Russell
Maysville, Ky.
9" Bottle
$195.00

Flask
Maysville, Ky.
$800.00

A. McCarthey & Bro.
Maysville, Ky.
Height 8"
$1400.00

M.C.R.
Adverstising Jug (6")
Maysville
$300.00

57

Jane Lew Pottery

Lewis County, West Virginia

A man named Parker was the first to have the Jane Lew Pottery sometime in 1856 to 1870. Then it was purchased by Colvin & Son from Akron, Oh. There were two sons and a daughter in the Colvin family.[1] The products of this factory were milk crocks, stone jars, from one to twenty gallon capacity, stone jar churns, and water jugs. Prices were based on capacity. A gallon milk crock was sold for ten cents and jars from ten cents for gallon size. Water and plain jugs and churn jars were a little higher.[2] The ware was taken by wagon and delivered in Braxton County and Randolph County. Mr. Earl Jackson worked for the Colvin and Son Pottery in 1885. He went bankrupt and closed down, but at a later date came back and paid off all debts be owed and the plant was dismantled around 1918.[1]

Jane Lew Pottery was the very first commercial manufacturing enterprise in Lewis County, W. Va.[2]

Above is a picture of the old pottery building with some of the products stacked in front. Uncle Noble Colvin is standing in the doorway with "Uncle" Jim and Mrs. Colvin nearby. The wagon load of clay was from Broad Run, about 2 miles away. Bob Colvin is at the controls. Charlie Colvin is astride the horse standing in the road. Others in the picture are employees or people interested in having their picture "tooken."

— "Hillbilly," Sept. 1961

The above picture is 84 years old and belongs to John Henderson.

1. This notation was found in a churn when it was purhased in 1971 by R.H. Ralston, Sr., from a Mrs. Coleman, who operated an antique shop at Romine's Mill on the Clarksburg Road.

2. "Hillbilly", Sept. 2, 1961, Pg. 1. Jane Lew Pottery: 10 cents a Gallon, by Donee Cook.

Jane Lew
5 Gallon Churn
6 Hearts in Circle
$3000.00

6" Canning Jar
McCarthey & Bayless
$1800.00

2 Gallon Storage Jar
J.P. Parker
Rare Heart Design
Stencil & Freehand
$700.00

J.P. Parker
Stars & Cross
Jane Lew
$525.00

Jane Lew
5 Gallon Churn
S.A. Colin & Sons
$500.00

Dog Door Stop
Jane Lew
$2500.00

3 Gallon Jane Lew
J.P. Parker
Stars & Two Crosses
$4000.00

NORTHEASTERN U.S.

Crock
Flower Design
Harrington & Burger
Rochester, Ny.
$8000.00

Group of Floral Pieces, all from Rochester, N.Y.
Factories: I.E. Harrington Burger, Burger, Stezenmeyer
Top Row, Left to Right: $800.00, $600.00, $800.00, $600.00, $900.00
Bottom Row, Left to Right: $600.00, $800.00, $800.00, $600.00

Butter Crock
Man in Moon
No Mark
$3000.00

A.A. Company
1 Gallon
Wine Jug
$295.00

Lyons Crock
1 Gallon
$265.00

Fulper Brothers
2 Gallon
$295.00

John Burger
Rochester, N.Y.
2 Gallon
$700.00

Harrington-Burger
Rochester, N.Y.
Stylized Double Floral
Blurred, Unusol
$2000.00

N. Clark & Co.
Lyons
3 Gallon
Preserve Jar
$2300.00

Cowden & Wilcox
Harnsburg, Pa.
2 Gallon
$500.00

N.A. White & Son
Utica, N.Y.
2 Gallon
$495.00

Cowden & Wilcox
Harrisburg, Pa.
2 Gallon
$475.00

Savage & Rogers
Havana, N.Y.
3 Gallon
$800.00

W.P. Myres
Amsterdam
$300.00

Hart Brothers
Fulton, N.Y.
3 Gallon
$295.00

T.H. Wilson & Co.
1 Gallon
Harrisburg, Pa.
$1500.00

Whites Utica
1 Gallon
Stoneware with Bird Decor
$695.00 Each

64

Whites Utica
Fantail Bird Looking Back
4 Gallon
$700.00

Stencil Eagle Crock
5 Gallon
$800.00

Freehand Decorated
$400.00

J. Norton & Co.
5 Gallon
$1800.00

Cowden Plain Crocks
$75.00 Each

F. Stezenmeyer
G. Goetzman
$1800.00

Cobalt Jar
10"
$700.00

Sherbume Churn
C. Hart & Son
5 Gallon
$800.00

65

Whites Utica Churn
6 Gallon
$3000.00

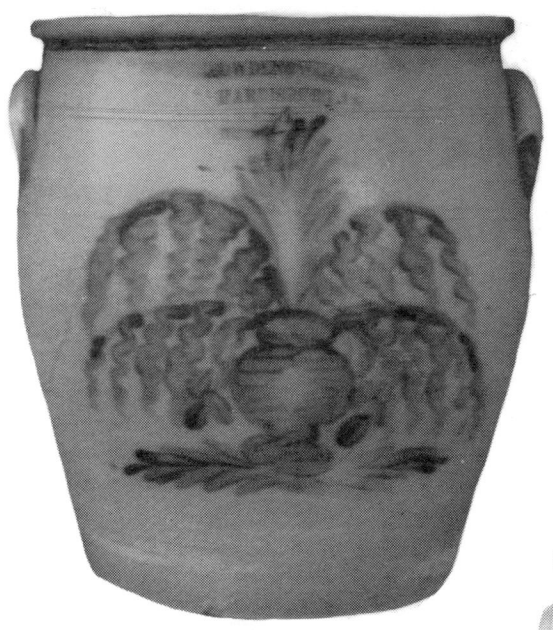

Cowden & Wilcox
Harrisburg, Pa.
Freehand Flowers
$3100.00

E. Norton & Co.
2 Gallon
$200.00

Ithica, N.Y.
3 Gallon
$400.00

Whites Utica Crock
3 Gallon
$500.00

Whites
Utica, N.Y.
5 Gallon
$600.00

Harrington-Burger
Rochester, N.Y.
Blurred
Double Floral
$1800.00

1 Gallon Jar
$295.00

Ithica, N.Y.
5 Gallon
$1500.00

Whites
Utica, N.Y.
2 Gallon
$495.00

C. Hart & Son
Sherburne, N.Y.
2 Gallon
$75.00

Cowden & Wilcox
Butter Crock
Harrisburg, Pa.
$150.00

Anchovisch
1 Quart Jar
Incised
$250.00

Potty & Flower Pot
$40.00

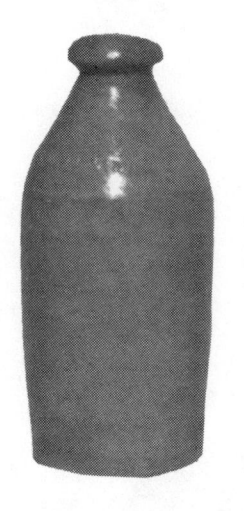

Cowden & Wilcox
Bottle & Jar
$200.00 Each

3 Gallon (11" H.)
Slip Quill Chicken
New York
$2100.00

Mabbett & Anthone
2 Gallon
Poughkeepsie, N.Y.
$595.00

Sipe & Sons
Williamsport, Pa.
2 Gallon
$250.00

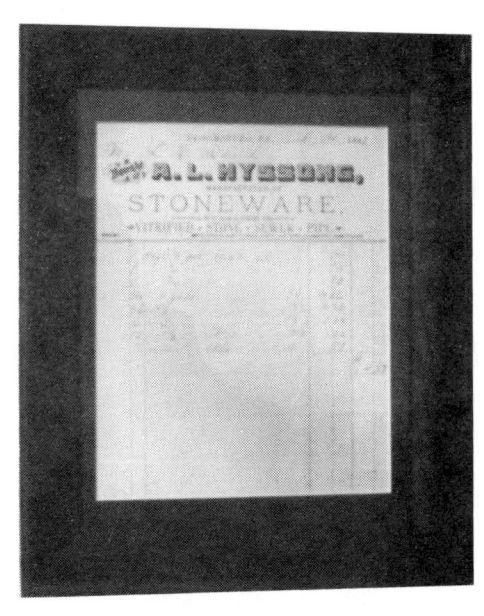

A.L. Hyssong
Manufacturer of Stoneware
Bloomsburg, Pa.
1892 Receipt
$150.00

Stoneware Receipt & Letter
Salamander Works &
Phoenix Pottery
Henry & Van Allen
Albany, N.Y.
1846: $725.00

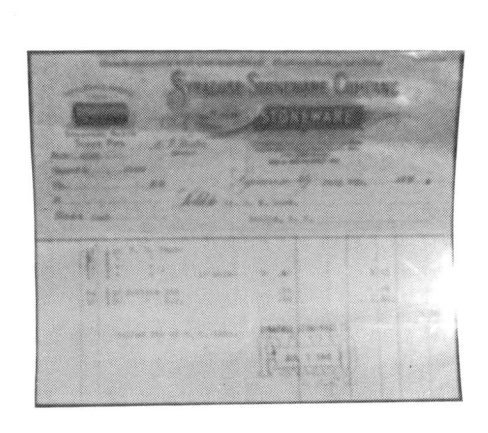

Syracuse Stoneware Co.
Receipt
$150.00

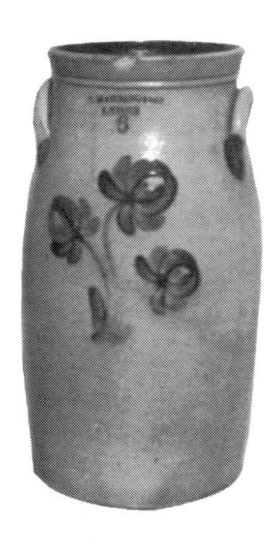

T. Harrington
Lyons Churn
6 Gallon
$800.00

F.H. Cowden
Harrisburg, Pa.
Pitcher
$1800.00

Cake Crock
5" Height
Maryland
$500.00

Butter Crock
1 Gallon
$450.00

69

Butter Crock
6 Quarts
$675.00

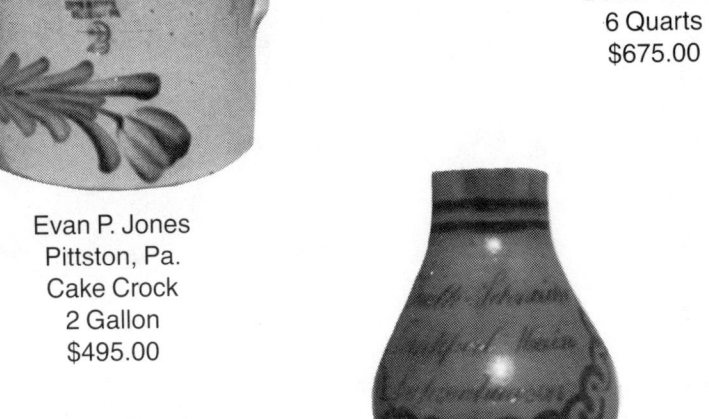

Evan P. Jones
Pittston, Pa.
Cake Crock
2 Gallon
$495.00

Sipe Nichols & Co.
2 Gallon
$650.00

A.G.C. Dipple
Lewistown, Pa.
Milkpan
$295.00

German Pitcher
3 1/2 Liter
Dauth-Schneider
Frankfurt, Me.
Sachenhausen
$750.00

Pitcher
Height 9"
$250.00

J. Burger Jr.
Rochester, N.Y.
5 Gallon Churn
$800.00

M. Woodruff
Cortland
Water Cooler
$2500.00

Butter Crock
2 Quarts
$355.00

P.A. Spittoon
$425.00

Pitcher
2 Quarts
$2200.00

S. Hart & Son
Fulton Churn
5 Gallon
$425.00

A. Seymour
Rome Churn
2 Gallon
$350.00

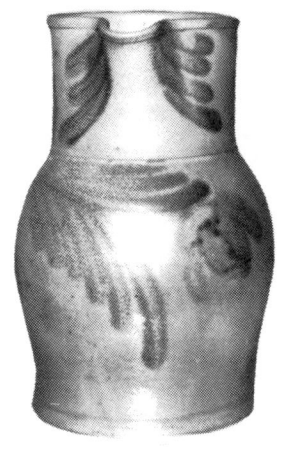

Cowden & Wilcox
(Stamped - 11")
Cobalt Decoration
$2095.00

Haxstun & Co.
Fort Edward, N.Y.
Churn
$800.00

Unmarked Churn
Canadian
Rare
5 Gallon
$3000.00

Fulper Pottery Co.
Ice Water Barrel
Flemington, N.J.
5 Gallon
$395.00

Cake Crock
2 Gallon
$495.00

6 Gallon Crock
Bird Design
C.W. Braun
Buffalo, Ny.
$3000.00

72

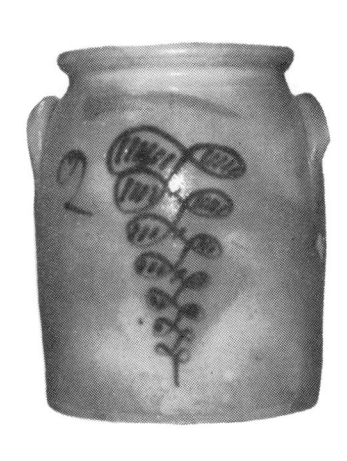

2 Gallon Jar
$295.00

S.T. Bewer
Havana, N.Y.
2 Gallon
$700.00

Penn Yan Jar
1 Gallon
$600.00

2 Gallon Jar
$800.00

Crock
A.O. Whittemore
Havana, Ny.
$15,000.00

N.A. White & Son
Utica, N.Y.
$400.00

J. Hart
Sherburne
4 Gallon
$250.00

N. White & Co.
Binghamton, N.Y.
2 Gallon
$450.00

J. Mantell
3 Gallon
$650.00

$350.00

John Burger
Rochester, N.Y.
2 Gallon
$575.00

Harts
Fulton Crock
2 Gallon
$600.00

W. Roberts
Binghamton, N.Y.
2 Gallon
$1200.00

Lewis Jones
Pittston, Pa.
4 Gallon
$450.00

Tall Storage Jar
2 Gallon
$195.00

Cooler
3 Gallon
$800.00

Tall Storage Jar
1 Gallon
$490.00

Cowden & Wilcox
Spittoon
$450.00

Double Love Birds
and "Centennial" in Blue
Boston Store Mark
$2500.00

Barrel Design Cooler
4 Spigot
4 Gallon
$225.00

M. Meal Portage Co.
4 Gallon
$120.00

75

Whites Utica (1 Gallon)
Bird on a Branch
$525.00

Cobalt Bird
$900.00

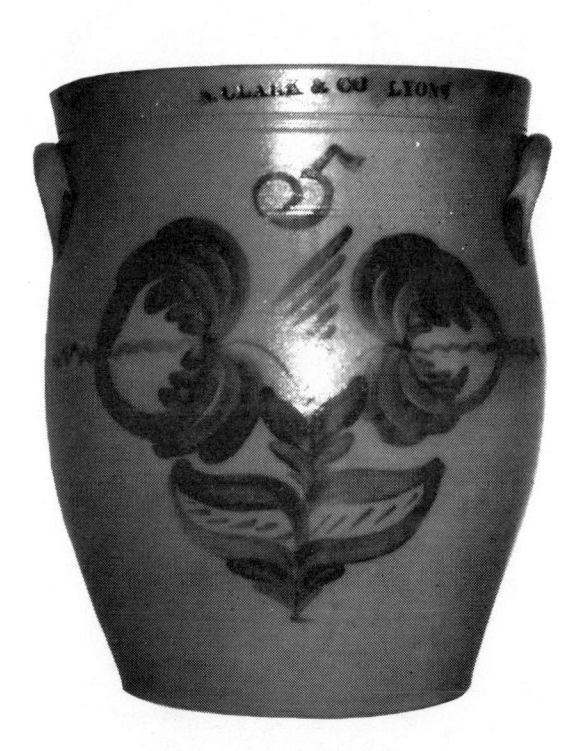

N. Clark & Co.
Lyons, N.Y.
5 Gallon Cream Pot
$2500.00

Harrington & Burger
Rochester, N.Y.
Elaborate Double Floral
Detailed Design
$2000.00

West Virginia

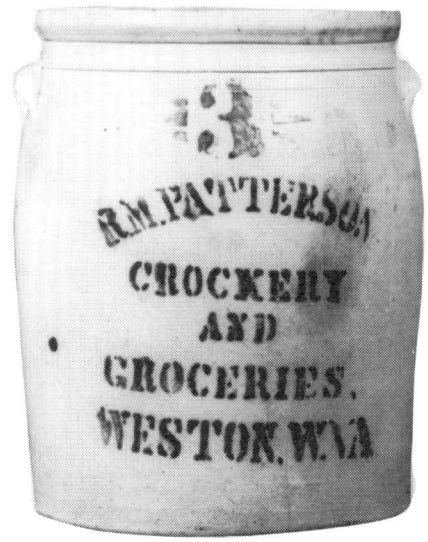

R.M. Patterson
Weston, W.Va.
Crockery & Groceries
3 Gallon
$275.00

Whiskey Jug
Advertising
Stencil, Cobalt
2 Gallon
$295.00

Knotts, Swandled & Co.
Palatine, W.Va.
2 Gallon, 11" Height
$495.00

George W. Johnston
Clarksburg, W.Va.
Freehand and Stencil
2 Gallon
$595.00

Whiskey Jug
Dated 1877
Palatine, W.Va.
1 Gallon
$195.00

Rager Lloyd & Co.
Palatine, W.Va.
18" Height
$2900.00

A.P. Donaghho
Parkersburg, W.Va.
10" Height
$350.00

A.P. Donaghho
Parkersburg, W.Va.
$500.00

6 Gallon Crock (20")
A.P. Donaghho
Parkersburg, W. Va.
$10,000.00

Haught & Co.
Shinnston, W.Va.
$395.00

Jugs

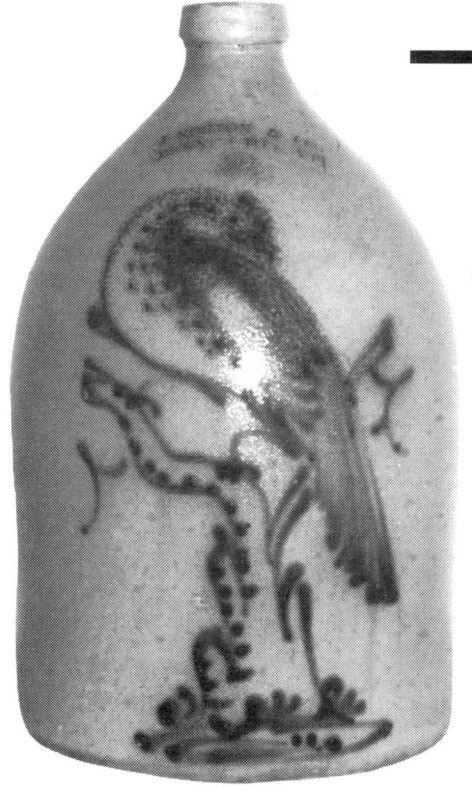

J. Norton & Co.
Bennington, Vt.
"Peacock on Stump"
$3000.00

W.H. Farrar & Co.
Geddes, N.Y.
1 Gallon Jug
$12,000.00

Stoneware Jug
Hamilton & Jones
Greensboro, Pa.
$295.00

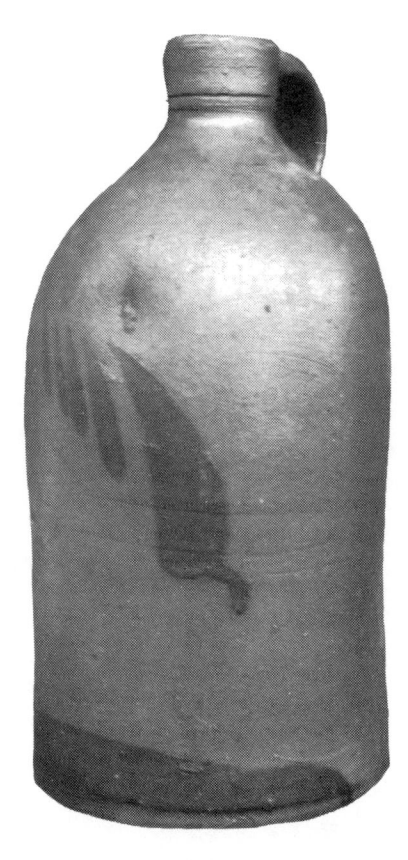

Stoneware Jug
$175.00

Whiskey Jug
Pittsburgh, Pa.
1 Gallon
$235.00

J. & E. Norton
Bennington, Vt.
$2500.00

5 Gallon Jug
Harrisburg, Pa.
$1200.00

Stoneware Jug
$295.00

Whiskey Jug
1 Gallon
$295.00

80

Pure Neversink Rye
1 Gallon
$250.00

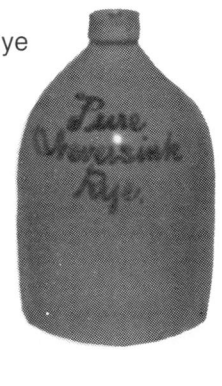

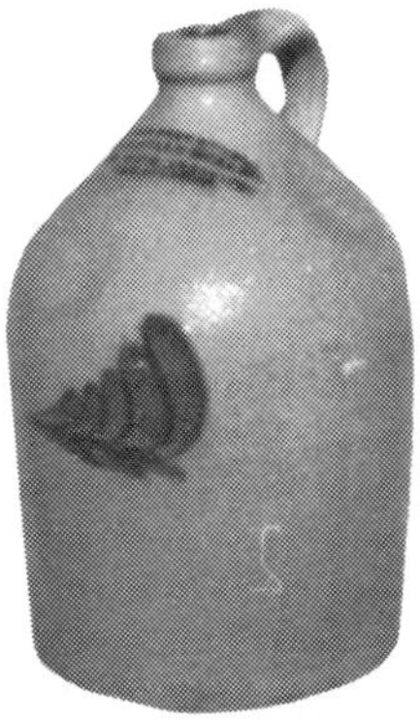

Jacob Pinkerton
Syracuse, N.Y.
1 Gallon
Wholesale Dealer in Wine
and Liquors
$350.00

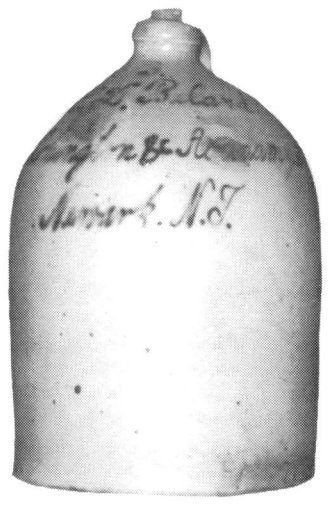

H.D. Beland (15")
3 Gallon Advertising Jug
Washington & Academy Ln.
Newark, N.J.
$895.00

I. Seymour
Troy, N.Y.
2 Gallons
$395.00

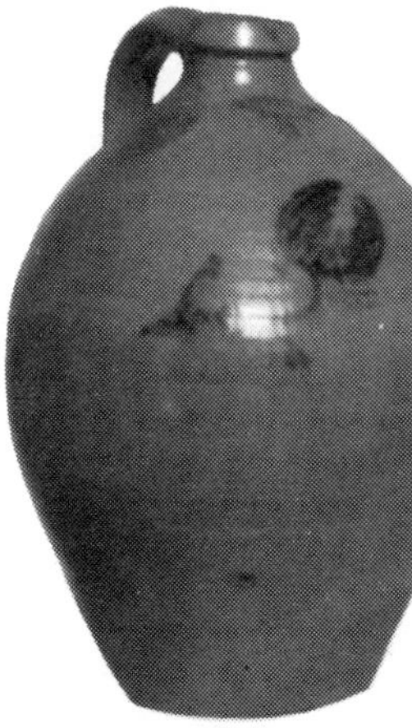

West Troy Pottery Jug
2 Gallon
$900.00

C. Hart
Sherburne Jug
2 Gallon
$450.00

W. Roberts
Binghamton, N.Y.
Butter Pail
3 Quart
$450.00

Jug
Bird on a Branch
$3000.00

81

Evan R. Jones
Pittston, Pa.
Butter Pail
6 Quarts
$900.00

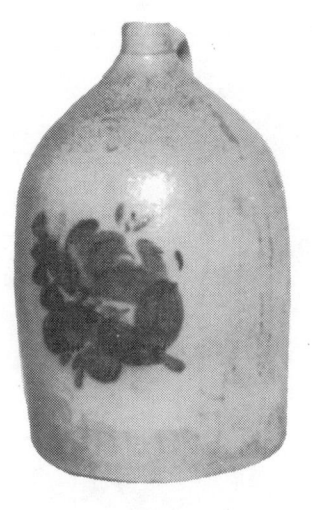

N.A. White & Son
Utica, N.Y.
5 Gallon
$395.00

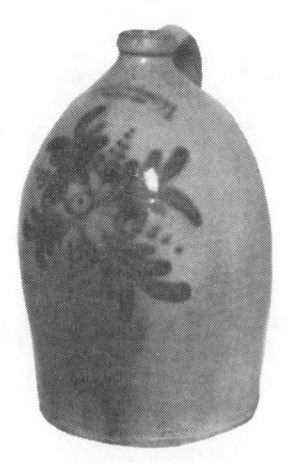

Cowden & Wilcox
Harrisburg, Pa.
4 Gallon
$650.00

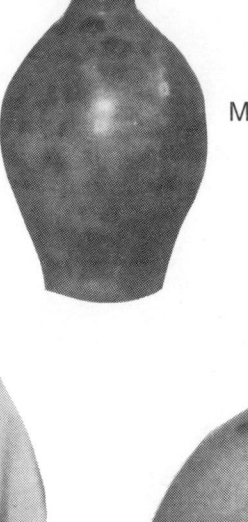

C. Crolius
Manahattan Wells, N.Y.
$1,000.00

R.A. Power
347 Grand Street
$295.00

Norton & M'Burney
Jordan
3 Gallon
Ovoid
$700.00

Cowden & Wilcox
Harrisburg, PA
2 Gallon
$450.00

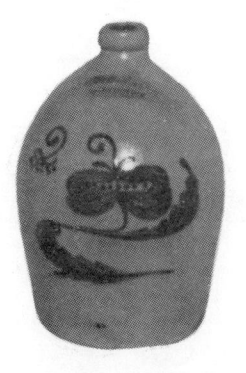

C. Phans & Co.
Geddes, N.Y.
2 Gallon
$350.00

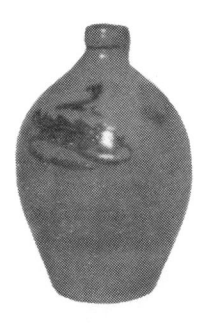

Clark & Co.
Mt. Morris, Pa.
2 Gallon
$395.00

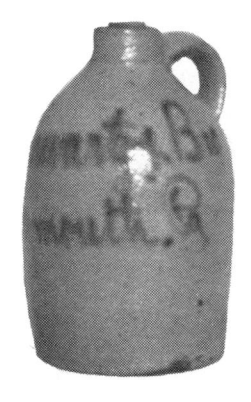

Fred Schwartz & Brothers
Plymouth, Pa.
2 Quart
$400.00

Large Spout Jug
1 Gallon
$225.00

C.H. Freeman
Corning, N.Y.
Syrup Jug
1 Gallon
$295.00

Whites
Utica
1 Gallon
$395.00

A.O. Whittemore
Havana, N.Y.
4 Gallon
$425.00

M. & T. Miller
Newport, Pa.
3 Gallon
$650.00

Whites Utica
Pinetree Decor
1 Gallon
$595.00

Stoneware Jug
$295.00

Whites Utica
2 Gallon
$350.00

I. Seymour
Troy, N.Y.
2 Gallon
$1500.00

John Burger
Rochester, N.Y.
2 Gallon
$450.00

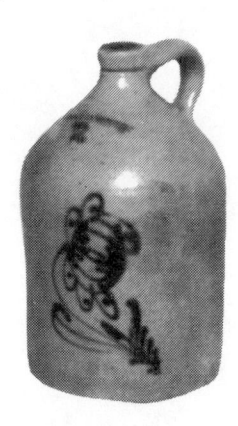

N. White & Son
Binghamton, N.Y.
2 Gallon
$495.00

Stoneware Jug
Slip Quill Design
2 Gallon
$325.00

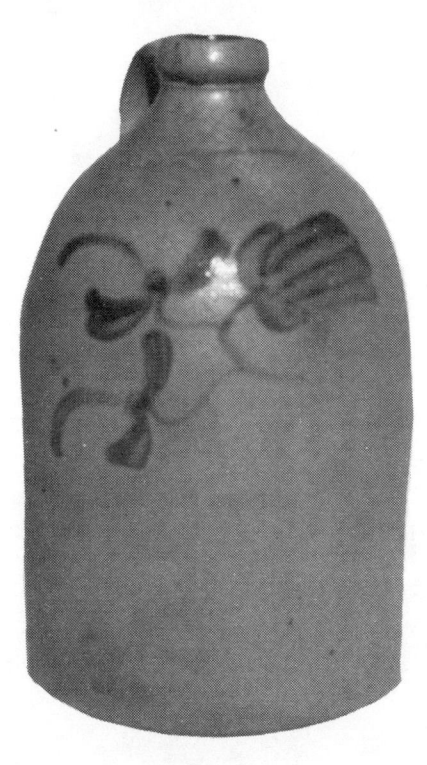

Hastings & Belding
2 Gallon
$350.00

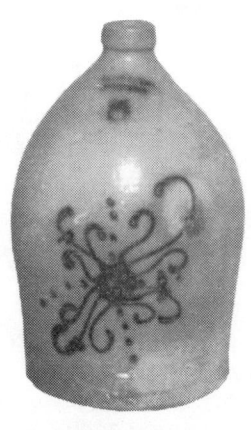

C. Hart & Son
3 Gallon
Sherburne
$400.00

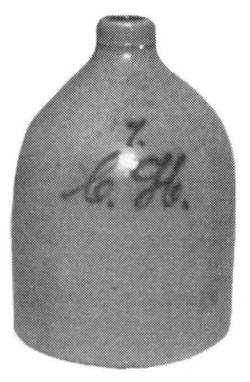

J. Fisher Jug
1 Gallon
$35.00

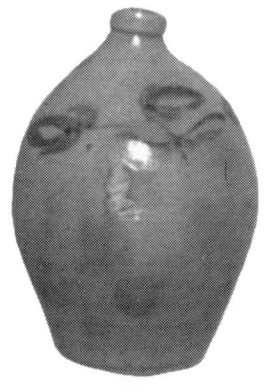

S.T. Brewer
Havana Jug
2 Gallon
$800.00

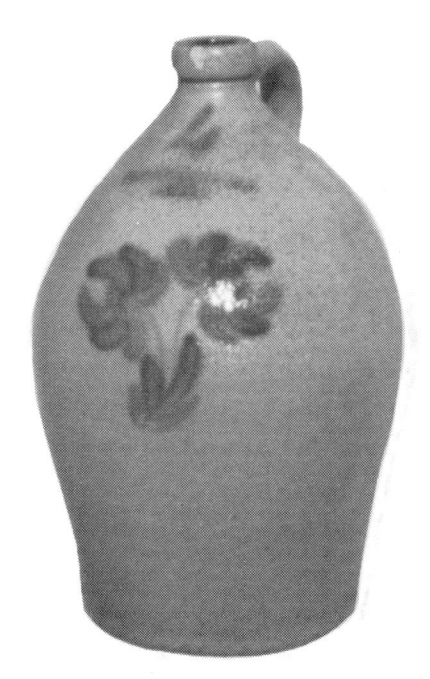

T. Harrington
Lyons
$395.00

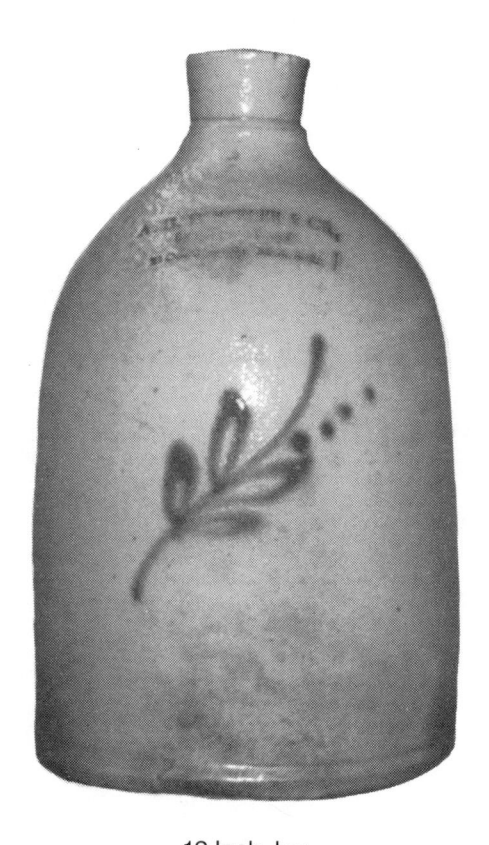

I. Seymour
Ovoid Jug
1 Gallon
$295.00

W. Roberts
Binghamton, N.Y.
4 Gallon
$750.00

T. Harrington
Lyons Jug
2 Gallon
$495.00

12 Inch Jug
Boston, Ma.
$1200.00

Ovoid Jug
No Mark
Tulip Freehand
$2100.00

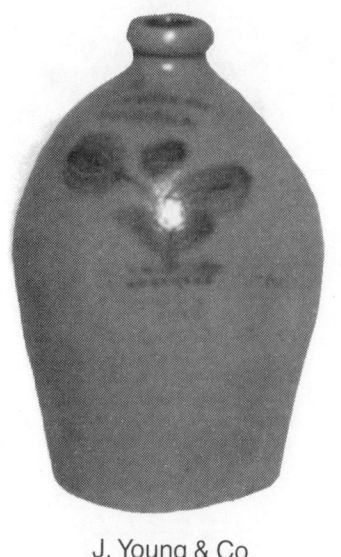

J. Young & Co.
2 Gallon
Harrisburg, Pa.
$675.00

Whites, Binghamton
1 Gallon
$250.00

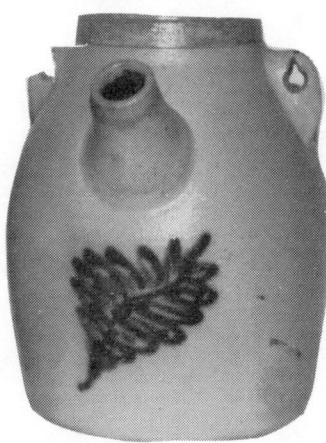

Unsigned Whites Utica
Batter Pails
Bird $1200.00
Oak Leaf $800.00

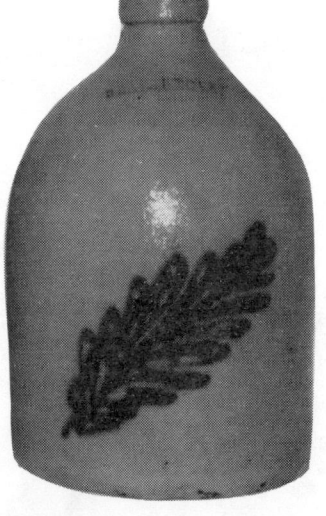

Whites Utica
1 Gallon Pine Tree
$900.00
Oak Leaf Decoration
$900.00

Whites Binghampton
2 Gallon
Double Poppies
$700.00

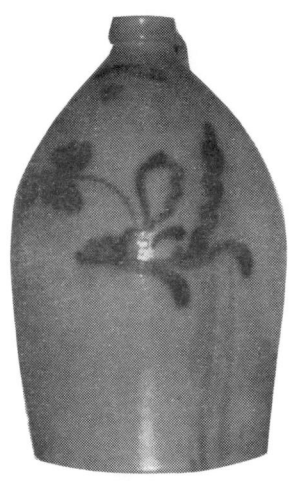

Cobalt Jug
13 Inch
$800.00

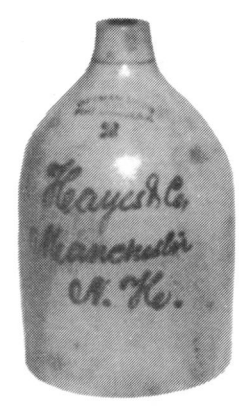

Ottman Brothers & Co.
Ft. Edward, N.Y.
Script: Heayes & Co.
Manchester, N.Y.
Advertising Jug
2 Gallon
$300.00

J. & E. Norton
3 Gallon
Bennington, Vt.
$295.00

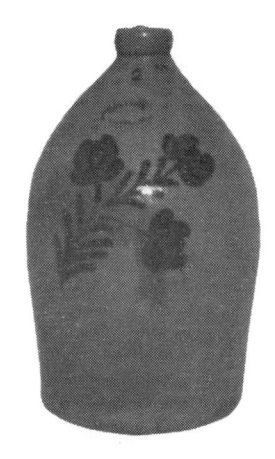

Sam L.I. Irvine
Newville, Pa.
2 Gallon
$700.00

Evan R. Jones
Pittston, Pa.
2 Gallon
$595.00

Nash & Co.
Abington, Ma.
1 Gallon
$195.00

Cowden & Wilcox
1 Quart Jug
$60.00

2 Quart Pitcher
$80.00

N. Clark & Co.
Rochester, N.Y.
Stylized Double Floral
Blurred
$2500.00

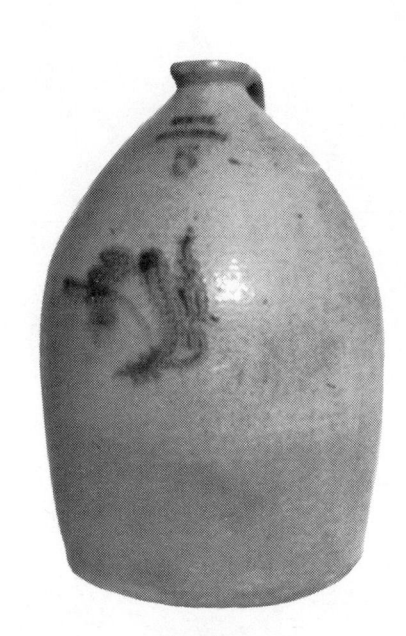

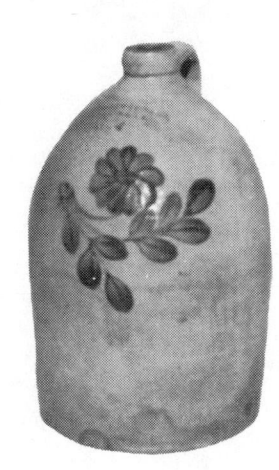

E.W. Farrington & Co.
Elmira, N.Y.
4 Gallon
$395.00

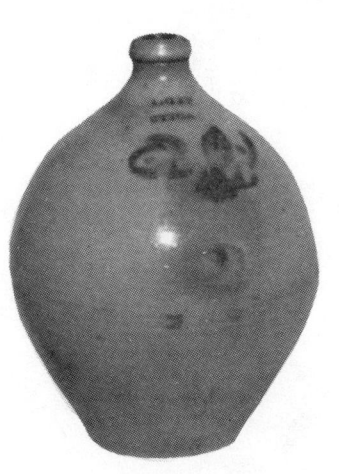

W. Hart
Ogdensburgh
5 Gallon
$350.00

A. Gay
Utica
2 Gallon
Ovoid
$350.00

Froehlich & Koehler
Newark, N.J.
11 Inch
$500.00

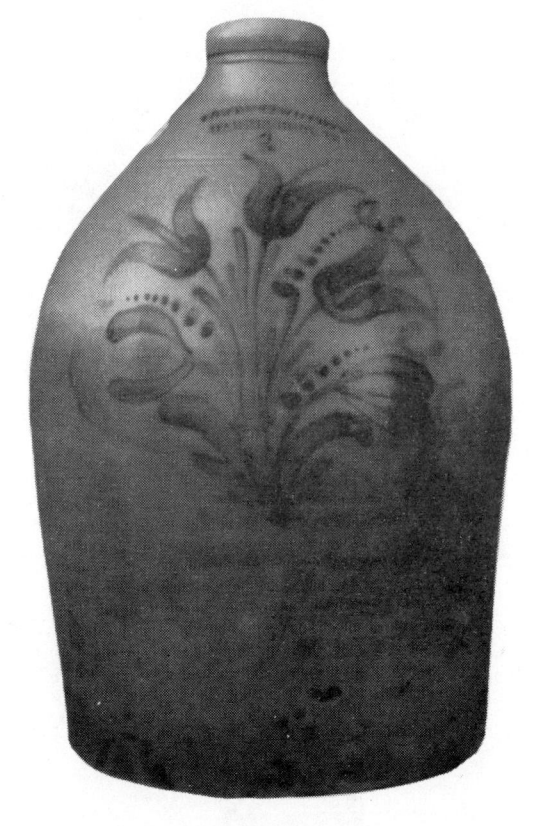

Stoneware Jug
Freehand Tulip Design
$800.00

16 Inch Jug
3 Gallon
Bird on a Branch
$700.00

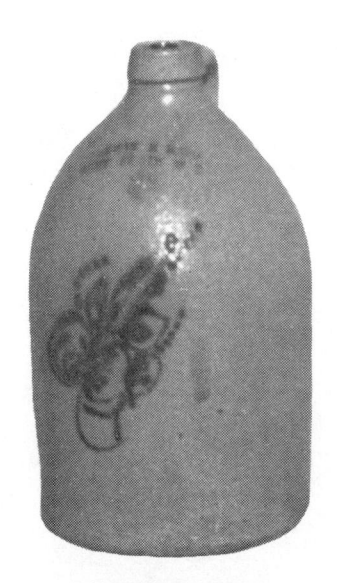

Darwin E. Reid
Fort Plain, N.Y.
2 Gallon
$280.00

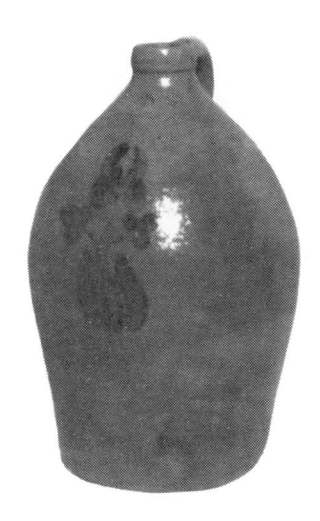

F.H. Cowden
2 Gallon
Harrisburg, Pa.
$350.00

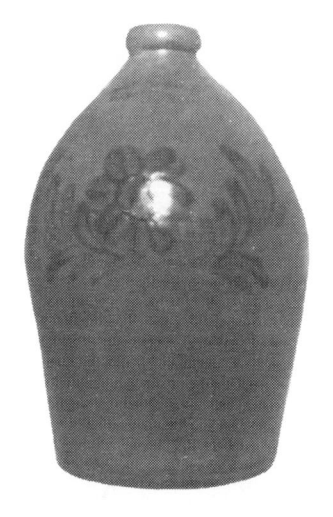

Cowden & Wilcox
Harrisburg, Pa.
2 Gallon
$600.00

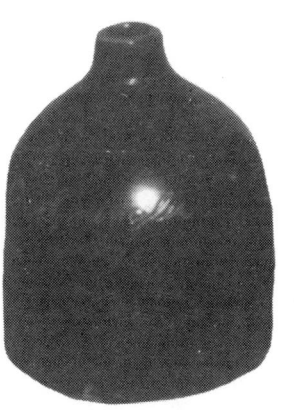

Albany Slip Jugs
2 Quarts
With Fred Farris
and A. Smingler
$75.00 each

Ithica, N.Y. Jug
2 Gallon
$395.00

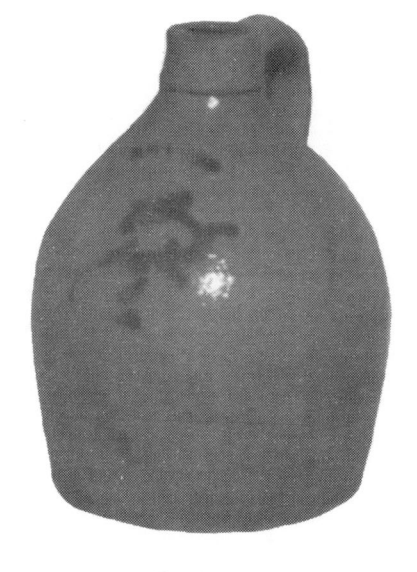

S. Hart Jug
1 Gallon
$350.00

Shelburne Jug
2 Gallon
$295.00

89

2 Handle Jug
James Hamilton & Co.
Greensboro, Pa.
Grapes, 4 Gallon
$5000.00

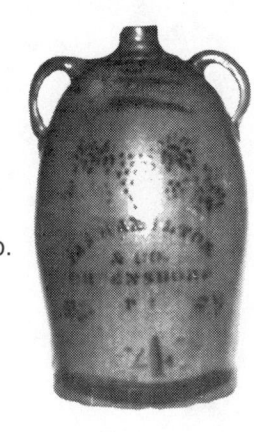

Hooded Chicken Waterer
1 Gallon
$300.00

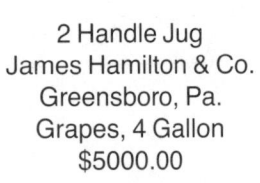

Sebb J. Beighel
Pleasant Unity, Pa.
1 Gallon Jug
$600.00

Harvest Jug
C.A. Hicks, 1885
Albany Slip Glaze
Scratch Decoration
$1200.00

Stoneware Jug
Hamilton & Jones
Greensboro, Pa.
2 Gallon
$300.00

R.T. Williams
New Genva, Pa.
5 Gallon
$700.00

Misc. Potters

Stoneware Pot
5" Height
$2500.00

T.C. Wilson
Clarion, Pa.
4 Gallon
$800.00

Stoneware Pitcher
8" Height
$4000.00

Stoneware Jar
Zanesville, Oh.
8" Height
$500.00

T.S. Balsley
Detroit, Mi.
4 Gallon
$450.00

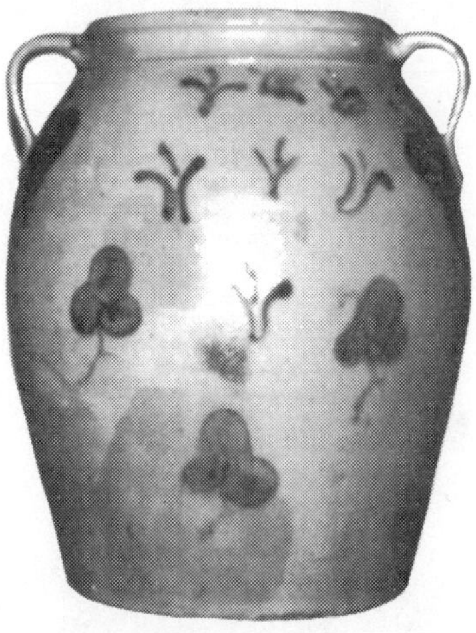

Cobalt Jar
Brownsville, Oh.
Turkey Tracks (H17)
$600.00

Crock (6½" x 10½")
1825
John Morgan
Baltimore, Md.
$5000.00

Churn
Freehand Decorations
Milwaukee, Wi.
$3600.00

Fred Kampfer
General Store
Clarington, Oh.
2 Gallon
$400.00

Pitcher
Freehand Decor, 14" Height
Baltimore, Maryland
$3000.00

P. & H. Jug
10 Liter, 16" Height
$700.00

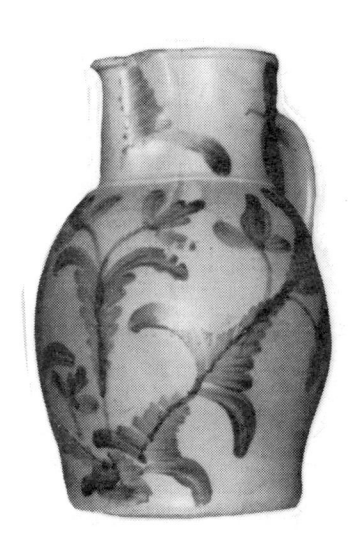

Pitcher, 14" Height
Ornate Freehand Decor
Shenandoah Valley
Potter Unknown
$3000.00

Stoneware Jug
Wheeling, W.Va.
$250.00

Water Or Milk Pitcher
E.I. Miller & Co.
Alexandria, Va.
Rare, $2200.00

Conserving Your Pottery

by Gene Green, Restorer

About two decades ago, I undertook the task of developing scientifically sound restoration techniques and materials to enable one to adequately restore any antique, regardless of material. My aim was to evolve a business for my family for generations to come. I was armed with an engineering and art education, as well as a broad knowledge of materials and their properties, particularly adhesives.

I began with pewter and similar alloys, then continued on to ivory, papier-mache, iron, marble, wood, cinnabar, and many others.

Fifteen year ago, I began the study of pottery, From an economic standpoint, pottery restoration showed little promise, as few people collected it, and prices paid for excellent pieces was quite low. Though it promised little in the way of income, the challenge to duplicate the many textures, such as unglazed red or tanware, the pebble grained salt glaze, and the sandy glazes were irresistible. The strength required would be extreme, when one considers that a water-filled twenty gallon weighs around 240 lbs. Should someone actually fill one, then be man enough to lift it, the failure of a replacement handle would be a disaster. Too many jugs and pitchers have been destroyed due to the failure of poorly attached replacement handles.

The lure of pottery is strong, and I've done little of anything else but study and restore it for years.

Over many years, some pottery pieces are subject to what is called "creep." The material is attempting to change shape, or flatten. This builds up extreme stresses in the piece. You've probably noticed that, some pottery, when broken, refuses to fit back together properly. On some pieces that are cracked, one side of the crack will stick out from the surface. In extreme cases, some will simply crack without being struck or subjected to temperature extremes. If a piece breaks when struck a minor blow, the blow was "the straw that broke the camel's back." The real culprit was the stressed condition of the piece due to creep. I plan to contact a ceramics related university in the spring with thoughts of developing a stress relieving cycle for pottery, should creep prove to be more of a problem to our pottery. The technology is presently available to determine if a piece is highly stressed. "Minor surgery" would be required on the piece.

After studying and restoring thousands of pieces, and hearing many "case histories" of damage, I offer the following information to help keep your pottery whole.

1. If at all possible, display pottery (or use dividers) so that contact between pieces is impossible.

2. Limit access by kids, pooches, and cats. Though unintentional, they take their toll.

3. Never handle pottery (or any other antique) by its handle. Handles, like the heads and arms of statuary, and other projections, are a "good ship in harms way," and are quite often restored, but often poorly attached.

4. When cleaning unrestored pottery, simply use a damp cloth. If the dirt does not come off, use the cleaning sprays found at the grocery. Paint and tar will come off with any methylene chloride stripper. Neither of the above will hurt the pottery. Acids should never be used on pottery, they will destroy redware, and tend to dull alkaline glazes. If cleaning of restored pieces can't be done with a damp cloth, it should be done by the person who did the restoration.

5. Do not use any abrasives, as some glazes are quite soft. Silicon carbide (wet or dry) grit is much harder, and will destroy any glass or glaze.

6. Rickety shelving units, or poorly installed wall shelves are a major destroyer of pottery. Buy industrial quality shelving units, then firmly anchor them to the wall. Have wall shelving installed by a professional. I know of one poor fellow who installed his own over the fireplace, only to have it fall, destroying numerous pieces of beautiful mocha.

7. Though Pottery looks great sitting near the fireplace, the uneven heat increases the stresses in a piece effected by creep. Avoid setting pieces near entry doors in winter.

8. When transporting pieces, select a box "that looks too big," and use plenty of packing. In winter, let it warm up slowly in the package before removing. A few pieces have failed by opening cold pottery in a warm area, so why take a chance. Try to diplomatically discourage others from handling your pottery. After having several pieces dropped in my shop over the years, I now block access to my work area.

Finally, you should be alerted to a possible health problem, should you buy a crock with caked contents in it. Though it is usually referred to as "Lime," and thought to be harmless, this is not necessarily true. Crocks were used to hold materials such as DDT, arsenic compounds, lye, lead carbonate (white lead), and other hazardous chemicals. Lime itself, when mixed with water, becomes "slacked Lime" (calcium hydroxide) and reacts on human skin or eyes the same as lye. When removing these materials, do so outside and carefully contain and discard them properly. Be sure to use eye, respiratory and skin protection while doing the work.

I hope that this article will serve to keep your pottery healthy. My thanks to my friend, Dr. Guappone for including it in his book.

Respectfully,
Gene Green
P.O. Box 162, Confluence, Pa. 15424
Phone (814) 395-5736

5 Gallon Crock
Beehive with Bees
Shuppes Bee Hive
Plymouth, Pa.
$1800.00

ORIGINAL PRICES OF STONEWARE

J. EBERLY & BRO.

Manufacturers of Stoneware
Strasburg, Shenandoah Co., Va.

PRICE LIST

Size	Price per Doz.
1/4 gal. Fruit Cans	$1.65
1/2 gal. Fruit Cans	2.40
1/4 gal. Jars	1.50
1/2 gal. Jars	2.25
1 gal. Jars	3.00
1 1/2 gal. Jars	4.50
2 gal. Jars	6.00
3 gal. Jars	9.00
4 gal. Jars	12.00
5 gal. Jars	15.00
6 gal. Jars	18.00
1/2 gal. Crocks	2.25
1 gal. Crocks	3.00
1 1/2 gal. Crocks	4.50
2 gal. Crocks	6.00
1/2 gal. Milk Pans	2.25
1 gal. Milk Pans	3.00
1 1/2 gal. Milk Pans	4.50
2 gal. Milk Pans	6.00

Size	Price per Doz.
Spittoons	$3.00
1 gal. Chambers	3.00
Jugs rate as Jars	
1/2 gal. Pitcher	2.25
1 gal. Pitcher	3.00
1 1/2 gal. Pitcher	4.00
2 gal. Pitcher	6.00
1/2 gal. cov. Jars	2.85
1 gal. cov. Jars	4.20
1 1/2 gal. cov. Jars	6.30
2 gal. cov. Jars	8.40
3 gal. cov. Jars	12.60
4 gal. cov. Jars	16.80
Water Coolers rate as covered Jars	
3 gal. Churns	12.00
4 gal. Churns	16.00
5 gal. Churns	21.00
6 gal. Churns	25.00

All Orders Promptly Filled

Goods warranted to give satisfaction

---

*The Shenandoah Valley Pottery A.H. Rice & John Baer Stoudt, pp. 74

FUTURE PRICES OF CROCKS

Dog Doorstop (7")
Named "Mikie"
$2000.00

New York Batter Pail
Fan Tail Bird
4 Quarts
$395.00

So far this year (1991) a jar with a dog on it sold for about $47,000.00. I attended an auction where a jar with a house and two trees sold for over $11,000.00. At the Bud Behm auction in Waynesburg, Pa., a 20 gallon jar sold for about $9,000.00. So if you think prices of stoneware are increasing now, just watch future sales. One other reason for the increase in prices, is that, exceptional stoneware is becoming more difficult to find and is remaining in collections. Years ago I sold part of my collection, but I would never do that again. If you have an opportunity to purchase a beautiful decorated stoneware jar, buy it and keep it in your collection, you will never regret it. you can never pay too much, for its value will increase far above what you paid. A few years ago I purchased a Maysville, Ky. butterchurn and everyone at this auction thought that I paid a very high price. So did I at the time, but it was beautiful. You could not buy it now for ten times that amount. In fact it is just not for sale.

When I published my first book, a price and reference guide, everyone began buying and selling stoneware. This happened in 1975 and ever since then stoneware has increased in value. It will continue to increase in value for many years to come.

I have several stoneware jars that are very exceptional and I cannot place a value on them. Several collectors who have visited my home always ask me to name my price. Once I wrote that there are nicer things to have than money and beautiful stoneware is nicer to have than money — isn't it?

Many collectors have collected all of the books that I have published concerning stoneware. They are pictorial price guides and all have different photographs. Each book is different and the opportunity to see the change in value is visible. The following books are still available from Guappone Publishers.
(1) *New Geneva and Greensboro Pottery* ($19.95)
(2) *Utilitarian Folk Pottery* ($24.95)
(3) *United States Decorated Stoneware* ($24.95)

Thanks

The "Clara Bell Antiques"
Elvin R. Culp & Frances (Jerry) Culp
(614) 454-2884   452-0950
Hull - Owens - Roseville - Rookwood - Weller Pottery
Blue-Decorated Stoneware - Clocks - Primitives - Heisey - Cambridge Glass
4868 East Pike, Zanesville, Ohio 43701

Vicki and Bruce Waasdorp
"Specializing in Antique Decorated Stoneware"
(716) 759-2361
Decorative and Investment, Authenticity and Full Satisfaction Guaranteed
Call or write to receive our latest offerings of Stoneware for sale.
P.O. Box 434, 10931 Main Street, Clarence, NY 14031

Winchester Antiques and Collectibles
Jerry and Jeanne Shobe, Owners
(703) 667-7411
Specializing in Stoneware and Furniture • 10:00 a.m. to 5:00 p.m. Mon. - Fri.
1815 S. Loudoun Street, Winchester, VA 22601

The George Wood House
(606) 759-7406
Washington, Kentucky 41096

Dr. Carmen Guappone with Gary Thomas, Potter
Thomas Pottery, First & Main, Fredericktown, Pa.

Jerry & Jeanne Shobe
Winchester Antiques, Winchester, Va.

Lantz Reppert, Virginia
Formally from Greensboro, Pa.

Joe R. Pyle, Auctioneer
Morgantown, W.Va.

Stoneware Auction, Organ Cave, W.Va.
Small Stoneware pitcher sold for $5,500.00

Dr. Carmen Guappone and Bernie Bales
at Organ Cave, W. Va. Stoneware Auction

Michael Culp
Clara-Bell Antiques, Zanesville, Ohio

99

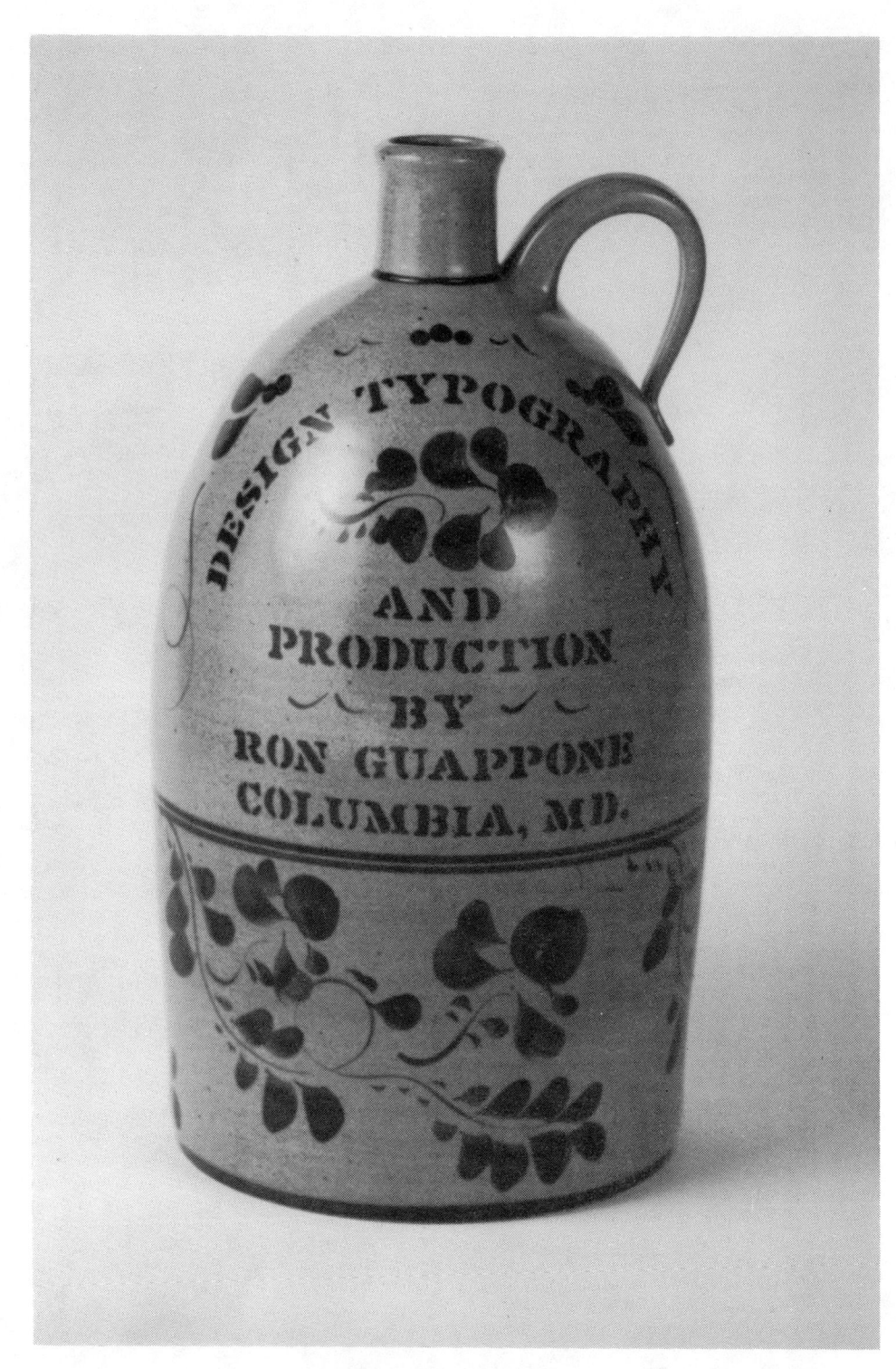

Made by Thomas Pottery
Fredericktown, Pa.